In Pursuit

of

Carp and Catfish

by

Kevin Maddocks

BEEKAY PUBLISHERS

. . . after 1½ hours every muscle in my body hurt

. . . and all these big fish for so little effort.

. . . clad in polished plates of bronze.

. . . quite possibly it had never been caught in its life.

. . . strangely enough, on both occasions it took the bait the second it hit the bottom.

. . . we excitedly carried the fish up the bank — my first twenty.

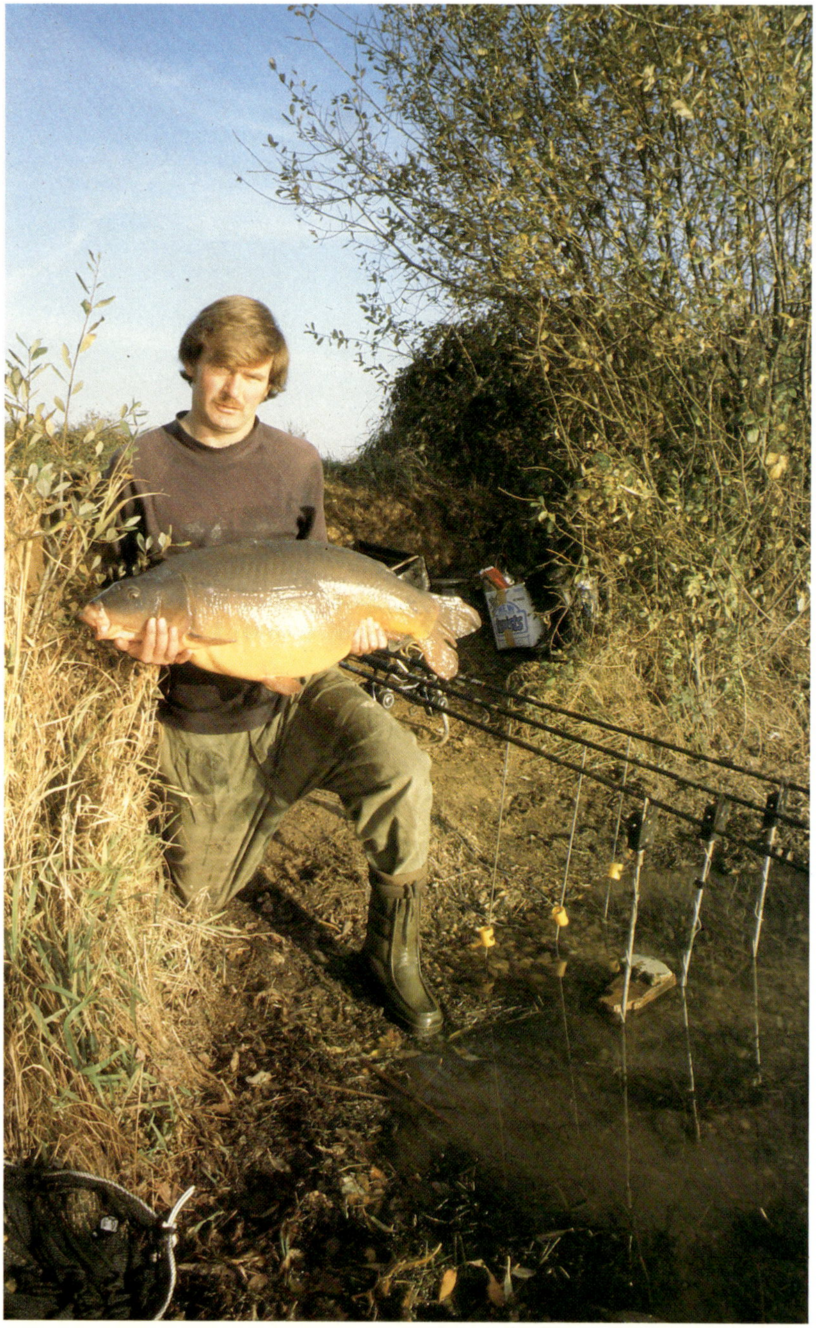

Like two young kids we convinced ourselves that it was huge.

... *'Meadow Magic'.*

There was no alternative but to hand-line the fish the last few yards to the net.

Failure or Success?

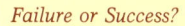

. . . whilst fishing from Greenbanks I hooked what appeared to be an eel.

. . . one hell of a handful!

... *dawn feeder.*

... *more 'Meadow Magic'.*

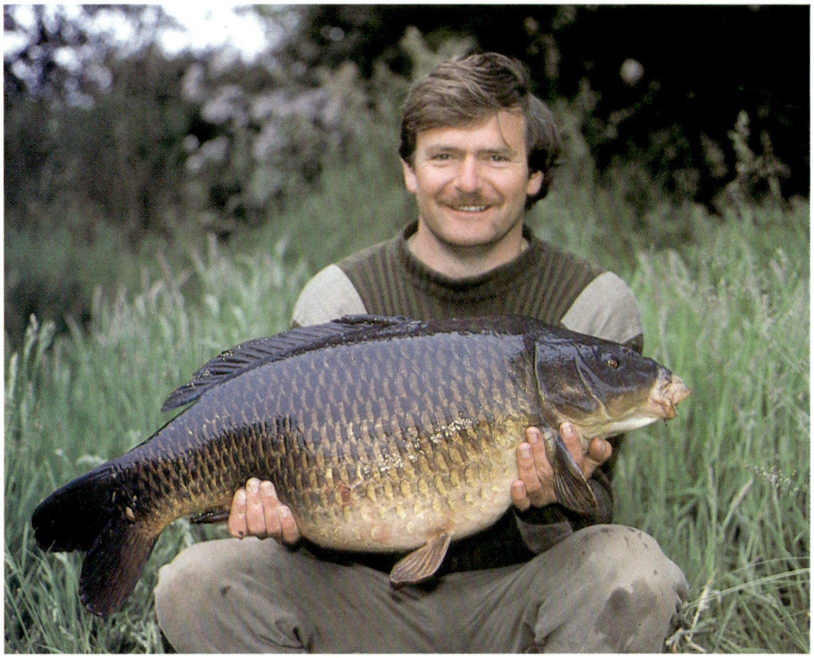

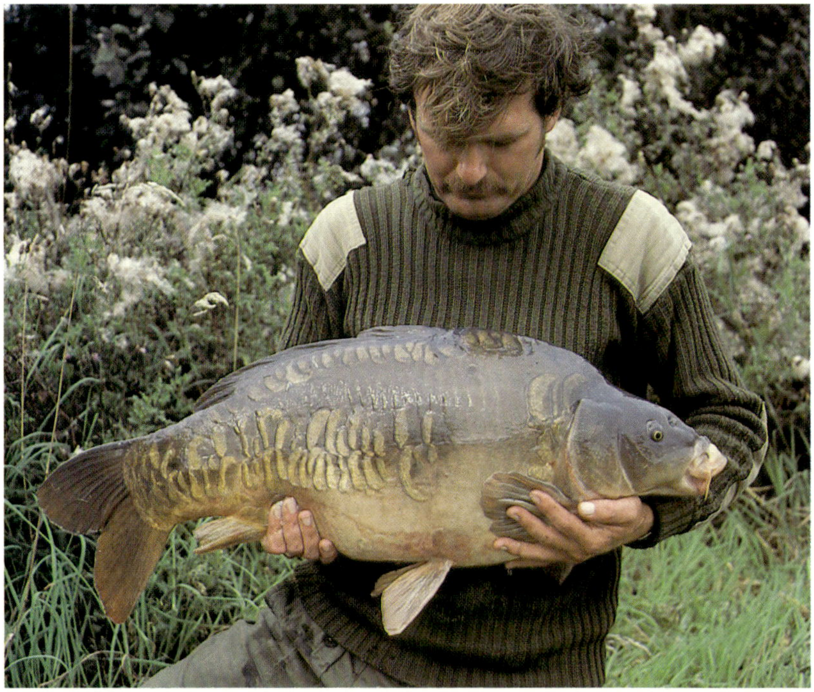

. . . one of the Waterways beauties.

. . . it was far from good looking but at 50 years old I handled it with great care.

Without a doubt, this was the best looking fish in the lake.

. . . Bob with 'Trees' plus our first 'neglected giant'.

. . . it was quite some time before I accepted the weight.

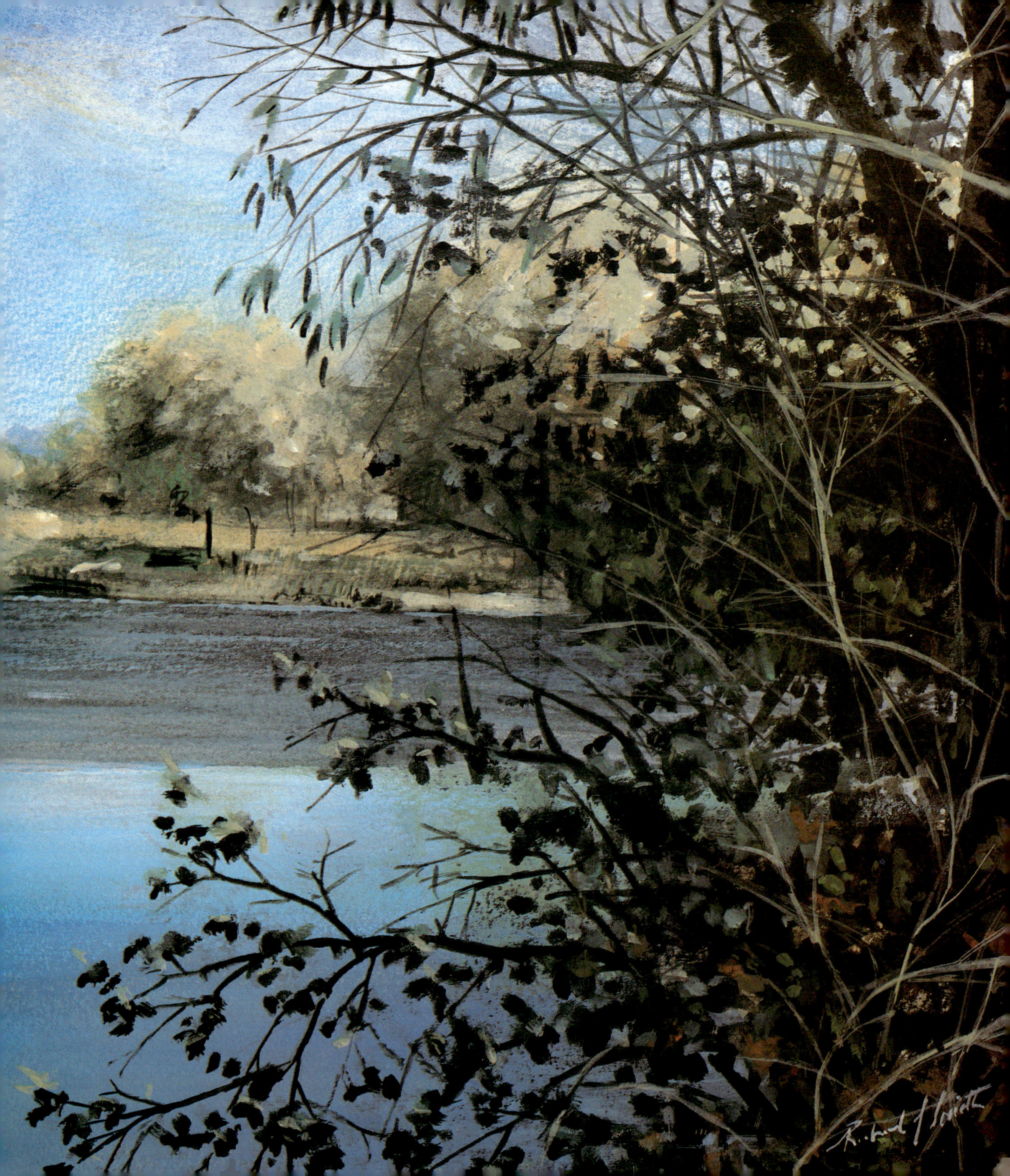

Meadow Magic

All too quickly, November had arrived once again and the short, glorious Summer season was no more. My quest, throughout the warmer months of '84, had been exclusively for that most mysterious fish, *Silurus glanis* — the European catfish. For two summer's long I had angled in earnest for this powerful, monstrous creature until the cooling waters had brought about a decrease in this fish's activity and hence turned my thoughts to mighty carp.

    I arrived at Meadow Lake on a cool, crisp Thursday morning — a traditional carp catching day during the 14th and 15th centuries when the monks set about catching a carp or two. What fun they must have had trying to catch the 'Friday Fish', as the monks called them and here was I, six hundred years on, accepting the same challenge. There were two differences, though; the monks fished for food which they usually caught, whereas the rest of the syndicate had failed to put a single fish on the bank from this water in this particular year. A few days earlier however, I had broken our bad run and on my first short session at the lake I landed the season's first carp; an immaculate common, weighing 22.14, from the Climbing Tree swim. This was, perhaps, the most difficult water I had ever fished with only 3 or 4 fish caught each year. It was even harder than Ashlea. The reason was obvious enough; the 8 acre water contained only about 20 carp and was so rich in food that the fish needed no angler's baits.

    I decided to fish the same spot again and during my two journeys along the fence bank, with the large amount of gear necessary for a three day session, I was enveloped by thoughts of how beautiful the lake must have looked in the summer. Huge weeping willows fringed the margins, extensive colourful lilies harboured the lake's huge fish and the clear, weedy water was enough to make any angler long for the big one. These were only thoughts though, for now the place looked old and weary. Leaves had left their branches and the water was a thick brown colour. Bare were the willow fronds and gone were the lilies. However, after 15 years of carp fishing my instinct told me that this change in the seasons was not as bad as it looked and made much less difference to the fish than to their environment, and my thoughts of summer went no further.

Although I had used an enormous amount of stealth in setting-up my pitch it was a little depressing to know that the carp were already aware of my presence. The behaviour of the resident wild life was enough to tell them that an angler was encroaching on their privacy — mallard and tufted duck would quickly vacate the area and the wild geese would honk and flap their wings to depart for pastures new. As if that wasn't enough, the pigeons clumsily fluttered their way through the branches, whilst coots and moorhens hid under marginal cover.

My 'noisy' arrival was completed at 9 a.m. by which time I had carefully groundbaited three areas of clean gravel with tiger nuts and was happy that all rigs had been set-up properly and positioned carefully. Tree top observation during my limited summer trips to the water had taught me that a bait positioned on the fish's most popular gravel bars was simply not good enough. All the carp I had seen feeding had done so only on the sloping edge of these bars. As I have already said, this was an incredibly difficult carp water, and it was therefore essential that everything was done correctly, especially the exact positioning of hook baits. I knew the contours of the swim very well and it was simply a matter of casting on top of the small areas concerned and gently pulling back until the terminal tackle could be felt to be inching its way down the gravel slope, an easy task when the behaviour of the fish is understood and the swim well known, but an impossible one for those unfamiliar with the lake. Unlike most of those who fish this old gravel pit, I always felt 'at home' here — it was my sort of water and the enormous success I'd had there compared with others gave me great confidence.

Most of the people who had previously fished the lake eventually gave up dejected and fishless; this was no ordinary carp water. With only twenty carp in eight acres, most of them uncaught, the size of many of these fish was sheer speculation. Huge carp had been observed on many occasions; one of these was probably well over 40lbs and fish below 20 pounds were quite rare.

As the afternoon passed and darkness approached my thoughts drifted to all fat things; catfish, carp and my pregnant wife! Our baby was due in four weeks time and I wondered about phoning home but decided not to. My baits were positioned absolutely perfectly and I didn't want to change that. I'd chosen very hard baits which meant that I only needed to re-cast every 24 hours or so. I planned to sit tight and await events.

Just as darkness fell there was a huge crash out in the centre of the lake as one of the big carp vaunted its freedom. A little later another jumped, this time along the margins to my left. It was very unusual to see carp jump on this water and it was obvious to me that the night was right; carp leaping in this kind of water had almost always indicated feeding fish in my experience.

Every minute of the first four hours of darkness seemed like an eternity — other fish had jumped, it was warm with a low air pressure and I was expecting one of the indicators to burst into life at every moment. I must have had six mugs of hot tea while I continually racked my brains over the way I was fishing — it had to be right if I was to be able to take advantage of this unique opportunity. Then, at 8pm, it happened; something had carefully picked up the bait on the centre rod but the fixed two ounce lead had scared the living daylights out of it and line poured off the spool at an alarming rate. There was a huge swirl some 25 yards out into the lake as a big fish made its bid for freedom. From then on the fight was rather slow and dogged so I shouted for my good friend Paul who was fishing the other end of the lake.

He was soon at my side and the fish was now close to the margins, but hugging the bottom. I told him that it was a big one and we both got very excited — could it be the very big one that some members had seen? The large landing net was sunk in position and although I managed on several occasions to get the fish up off the bottom it was reluctant to show itself in the darkness. Paul was worried about his lack of netting experience but I knew he could keep a cool head so I suggested that he use my dull pocket torch to be able to determine the right moment. With the weak beam of the torch trained at the surface I heaved the fish to the top and as it rolled we both saw its huge flank glisten. As the carp made its final run, taking a little line off the clutch, we both speculated on how big it might be. Like two young kids we convinced ourselves that it was huge. A minute later it was all over, the big shining bulk was in the net and in a short time our hearts could stop pounding. We quickly shone the torch on the fish which, sure enough, was a big mirror, but as I lifted it ashore it became apparent that this was not the one we had hoped for. The immaculate mirror weighed in at $32\frac{3}{4}$lbs; a big fish but no monster, although it equalled my best taken from the lake some two years before. After a celebration cup of 'liquid gold', Paul returned to his pitch.

    Not long after I had carefully re-cast all the rods another carp crashed out, this time only a few yards from the baited area. I stayed awake as long as I could but the toil of continuous hard work during the previous days made it impossible to stay awake all night. I positioned my bedchair as close to the rods as I could and decided not to set-up a brolly. A November night can turn bitter without warning but I didn't want anything to get in my way should another big fish take the bait during the night.

    Dawn came and the first ritual of the day was successfully carried out despite damp matches. Determined not to disturb the swim, I left the rods well alone and sat back to enjoy the first cuppa of the new day and the thoughts of the big mirror we'd captured. From time to time I stood up and peered through the trees to see if Paul was up and about, and on one occasion I noticed his rod was well bent into a fish. I decided to go round to his swim immediately to see if I could be of any assistance but I got no further than thinking about it. Just at that moment the buzzer to my right hand rod sounded and I was immediately into another fish. I couldn't believe it — we'd hooked three carp in less than 12 hours on a water that hadn't produced a fish for 12 months! For some reason, my fish decided not to fight and within a minute or so I pulled a very big common over the net. Why it didn't fight is unknown to me, for in my four years on the water this particular fish had not been caught and quite possibly it had never been caught in its life. It was in truly excellent condition and it tipped the scales at 28½ pounds. My thoughts immediately returned to Paul so I quickly sacked the fish and hastily made my way round to his swim as I was sure he hadn't yet landed the fish. On arrival I was grieved to hear that his hook-link had parted on what appeared to be a big fish and inevitably such a big disappointment marred the capture of my big common for us both. Paul had fished many hours for such a chance and words cannot describe such a disappointing experience — only a carp angler knows how it feels.

The glorious calm, sunny day that followed offered poor conditions for the chances of further action and so we spent most of the day drinking cups of tea and chatting about the lake and its beautiful inhabitants. As the syndicate leader, Paul was very pleased that some fish had, at last, been caught and it helped alleviate that horrible gut feeling of losing a big fish. We talked for many hours about the huge carp that the lake possibly held and we speculated on how big the few stock fish, introduced two years previously, might now be. Then with darkness only an hour or two away, we separated for another lonely night in the hope that we might be rewarded with the capture of another of the elusive Meadow monsters.

For the last twenty years, scores of carp anglers had fished the nights at Meadow with the same result and this night proved to be no exception. However, it was not to be very long before Paul's yearning for knowledge of how the stock fish were faring was to be satisfied. At 8.15 that morning I had a run on the right hand rod and after a brief tussle landed a short, plump mirror. It was one of the stock fish which now weighed 15¾ pounds; an 8 pound gain in 24 months. Paul was 'over the moon' about how well the fish had done and he couldn't have wished for more from what turned out to be the last, and only, successful session of the season.

We fished a further day and night with no action and I continued to fish three days a week for the rest of the month but had not a single run — an example of the uncertainty of *real* carp fishing; an uncertainty which makes the sport so fascinating and magical.

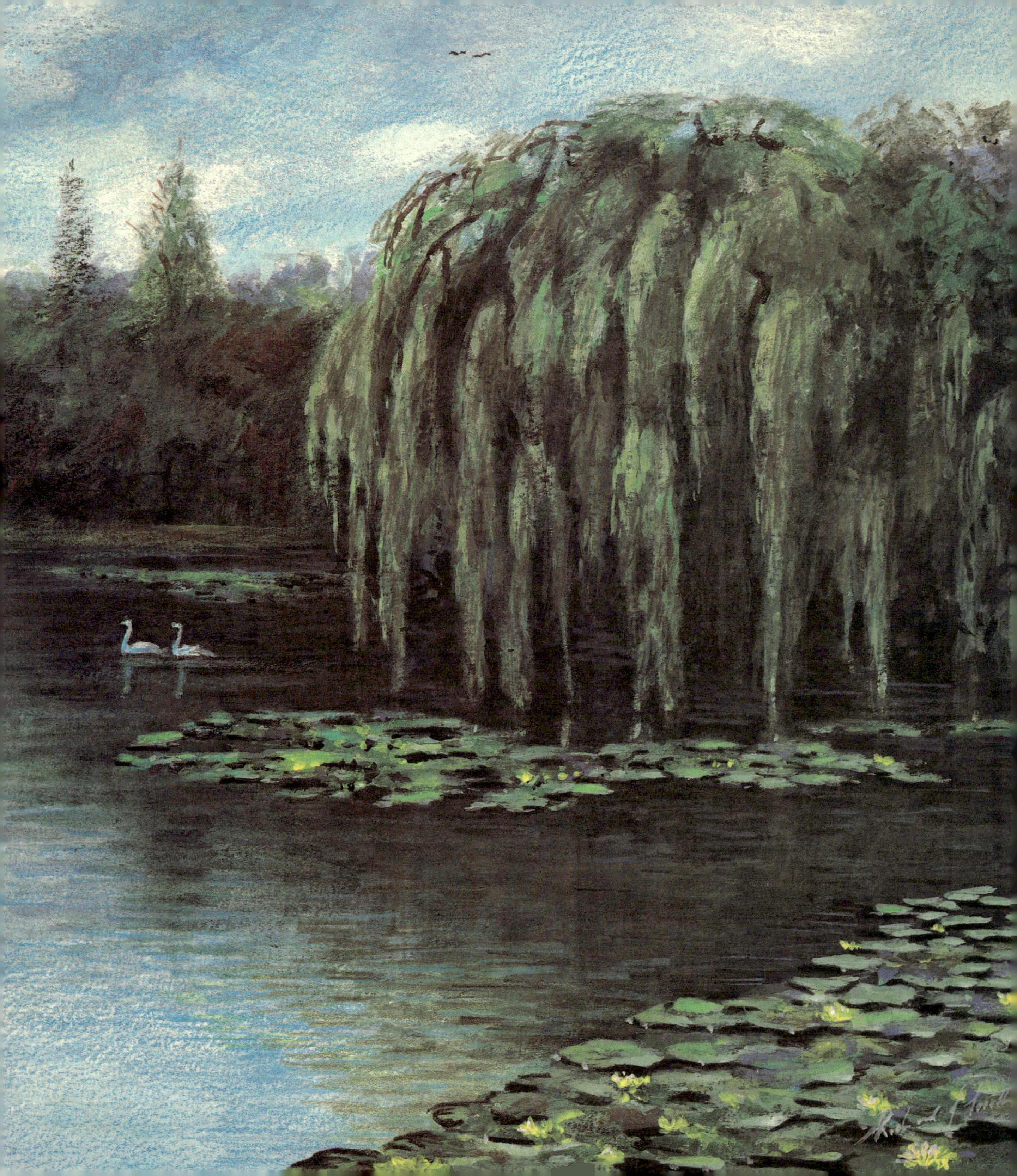

In The Beginning...

The 16th June 1970 was indeed one of the most significant days of my angling career, and it is perhaps best if I tell you the story.

At 4am my alarm clock burst into life and this was shortly followed by the second back-up alarm. As keen as mustard I leapt out of bed and within twenty minutes I was on my way to Vic Hull's house in Edmonton. As I turned the corner into his road, there was all his gear on the pavement; as always, he was ready and ahead of schedule. I strapped all I could onto the back of my AJS 500cc twin and with two rod holdalls hanging round Vic's neck we started on our 40 mile journey. The destination was Woburn Abbey in Bedfordshire. Woburn is a beautiful private estate and the lakes are typical of waters constructed in the grounds of a stately home. Anyone who has seen lakes of this kind will know what I mean.

It had taken us an hour to get there which wasn't bad considering the discomfort we had to put up with on our fishing expeditions. Just imagine the situation; strapped to the petrol tank and pushing hard against my chest was my tackle bag and seat — this made steering a little on the difficult side to say the least. Against my back was Vic leaning forward fighting the wind resistance caused by the two rod holdalls strapped to his back. We had on previous trips attempted to tie the holdalls to the side of the bike but being six feet in length they interfered with the steering so much that on one occasion we went straight on at a bend! Also strapped to Vic's back was his kit bag and on the rear of the motorcycle was the rest of the gear; Vic's seat, food bag, clothing bag, etc. I remember that I was always getting at Vic to keep his kit down to a minimum but he insisted on keeping everything in separate kit bags. Still, what had I to complain about? Vic, who was nearly 30 years older than I, had introduced me to fishing and used to pay for all my permits, petrol money and even some of my tackle. This was a godsend, for my first year of fishing was whilst I still attended school, only then to be followed by six years of low wages whilst serving an apprenticeship. I really enjoyed fishing with Vic and I will always remember him for his generosity, good company and first class angling instruction.

That particular morning our quarry was golden tench and so we staggered with all the gear to the banks of the Lower Drakeloe lake where we had caught good bags of this comparatively rare fish on previous visits. The float tackles were soon set-up and within a short time Vic and I were contentedly fishing alongside each other. As is usual on all my fishing trips I was soon feeling very hungry but to my horror, I found maggots crawling amongst my sandwiches. Whilst I was picking the creepy-crawlies out from in between the slices I remember Vic saying, "Now you know why I have a separate food bag". Having a laugh didn't distract Vic from his float for he had noticed it tremble slightly and as it gave a little lift he connected with the first tench of the morning.

I was just as keen in those days as I am now and I remember perching on the edge of my seat hoping and praying for a bite, especially as Vic had already scored. The minutes seemed like hours but it wasn't long before my float leant over and gently disappeared into its own vortex. Two or three minutes under the strain of my three-piece cane Avon rod and the golden tench was in the net. Gleaming like a goldfish, the three pounder was popped into the keepnet and out went a little more bait. By mid-day we had caught two golden tench, two green tench, a 1lb crucian carp and a 10-inch rudd. Although we had taken much larger bags on previous trips we were still very happy. In fact Vic smiled happily for a whole hour following his capture of the crucian.

It was a pleasant day with little wind and as the bites tailed off I came out with one of our favourite statements. Often we used to say, "What I am going to catch now is . . ." and we would proceed to state what we'd like to catch. I must admit it did get a bit silly at times and as you can appreciate it rarely worked, but it all helped to make the day more enjoyable.

However, irritated by the sight of what appeared to be a rolling carp I said to Vic, "What I am going to catch right now is a four pound carp and it must be a common". It was a rather stupid statement because I never dreamed that I would ever catch a common or mirror carp and I had never seen anyone else catch one either. Uncannily, within a few seconds of that statement my float shot under and before I could strike I was into another fish. But this 'tench' fought a lot differently from the others — unlike anything I had ever caught before and after about five minutes Vic told me that it was almost certainly a carp, because of the huge 'boils' it was creating on the surface of the water. From that minute on the adrenalin really flowed and my heart thumped like mad and after a ten minute fight Vic managed to net the fish for me. Strangely enough it weighed 4 pounds and was a common. Little did I know then just what the capture of this carp would lead to; my quarry for at least the next decade had been chosen . . .

From that day on I constantly pestered Vic to take me somewhere where there were carp but all of the waters he fished contained none or very few. We had heard of a place called Waterways somewhere in Cambridgeshire that held a good head of tench and carp and so we devoted three complete weekends the following close season looking for the water. We visited lakes in the area where we thought it might be and fortunately we found it during the third weekend. The fishery was owned by a very eccentric gentleman solicitor who was deeply into the mystic arts, and it was run by his gardener (who was even more deeply into backhanders!). After a very tactful chat with the gardener, Joe Westwood, we were invited to fish as guests on three occasions the following season and if we behaved ourselves we were told that we might get into the syndicate the year after that. I will always remember that day — it was the most beautiful place I had ever seen; originally it had been just two ordinary gravel pits but it was now transformed by islands, lily beds and weeping willows and all set in well kept private grounds. We were stunned by its beauty, and not being able to have a look round, and after hearing that it contained massive carp and tench, we couldn't wait for the season to start.

During the remainder of the close season I tried to find out more about catching carp but, to no avail. Vic had caught odd ones on previous occasions and so we had a rough idea of what to do — or so we thought. One thing that Vic had discovered and which served us well for a long time, was a particular terminal tackle set-up. This rig is what we all accept nowadays as the standard link-leger. It consisted of a lead weight tied to a length of line about four inches long. To the other end of this link a swivel was tied. This was allowed to run along the main line but was stopped by another swivel about 18 inches from the hook. I remember asking Vic what the link was for and he didn't really know, except that it had worked better than all the other rigs he had tried. The reason I enquired about the link was because until this time I had always used the lead straight on the line when legering and it wasn't until a couple of years later that I realised what purpose the link served.

On the 1st July 1970 we were once again standing on the banks of Waterways but this time with our tackle. We had a good look round and I remember the vivid atmosphere of the place during that very first recce. Huge common carp, 'clad in polished plates of bronze', cruised in and out of the lily beds, around the islands and under the willow fronds oblivious of any spectators. As I watched these majestic fish I was left speechless — it was a sight I'd never seen before. I remember thinking that surely they couldn't all be impossible to catch for there were so many of them but how powerful they must be and what sort of fight they would put up if we were fortunate enough to hook one.

Perhaps fortunately for us, we hooked no carp that trip but we did catch two dozen tench and some nice roach and perch. Our second visit met with almost identical results and again no carp were tempted but the third trip was different . . .

It was August 8th and knowing that this would probably be our last guest visit for the year we were up bright and early and settled into our swims by 5am. Vic chose the 'boards' swim and I plumped for the 'point' which was only about 15 yards away.

It was quite an active morning for we were both busily catching tench but our carp rods remained motionless until midday. Vic was laying-on with float tackle alongside the willow fronds to his right when his huge piece of breadflake was picked up. Seconds later Vic's rod was bent double and his clutch was screaming. We had hooked our first Waterways carp. I immediately rushed round to Vic but it wasn't until thirty minutes later that I was able to slip the landing net under a beautiful 16lb common carp. This fish was so much bigger than anything else we had ever caught that it seemed impossible that we had ever landed it. The gleaming, closely-set scales made it so beautiful that we regarded the fish with awe: the Waterways commons were some of the finest looking fish in the country — and we had caught one.

We were fortunate enough to be able to persuade Joe to let us have one more trip that year but it wasn't until the following year, 1971, that we saw our next double figure carp.

Now that we were members of the syndicate we could fish whenever we liked so Vic and I decided to spend five consecutive days on the water in July in an attempt to connect with another of the hard fighting commons. Joe's son, who lived in a nearby village, kindly fixed us up with bed, breakfast and evening meal and getting to and from the lake was no problem on the motorbike especially as we were able to leave our gear safely at the water. In those days we never considered the possibility of night fishing.

It was a red hot week as far as the weather was concerned and as usual the tench were feeding with abandon. This suited us fine as we were quite happy to catch tench with one rod whilst we left the carp rod to fish for itself with a huge piece of flake. I know now of course that this is a most unproductive way to fish for carp, but at the time it was our accepted method because we wanted to catch other species too. At the crack of dawn each morning we were down the lake and at about 9am we used to go back to our digs for breakfast — if you could call it that; we got one small slice of rubbery toast and a stewed cup of cool tea, and if you think that's bad you should have seen the dinners! We were of course very disappointed about this but the good fishing helped make up for it with at least fifteen tench being landed each day. We seemed very unlucky with the size of our tench though, as they only averaged about two pounds and none were over three, but what we couldn't understand was how Fred, one of the other syndicate members, kept on catching four pounders. We accepted this for a while until one day he told us he'd caught a near five pounder which we noticed he had put into his keepnet. A little later Fred disappeared down the road for his usual mid-day pint so I seized the opportunity and nipped around to his swim with a set of scales. I promptly weighed the fish, which went 2 pounds 12 ounces so we then realised we were not being so unlucky after all.

    On the third day of our stay I decided to have a go in the lake we called the Bird Lake which until this time we had not fished and it was here that I had my first encounter with one of the Waterways carp. On looking around I noticed a huge gathering of carp at one end of the lake. Here the lake tapered down in width to a narrow bay and I would estimate that there were perhaps 100 carp in the small area, which, in fact, was probably the total population of the lake. I could not see one mirror amongst them — they all appeared to be commons; mostly doubles with the odd smaller and larger specimen. 'How could I fail', I thought.

    With shaking hands I flicked out a piece of freelined bread flake into the centre of the shoal and within a few minutes the line tightened and I was battling with my first double figure common. Anyone who has hooked these Waterways carp knows the tremendous speed that they shoot off at with the clutch screaming like mad. If your clutch was not adjusted correctly your line was smashed instantly no matter how high the breaking strain. After what seemed an incredible fight I netted the fish which turned out to weigh 12 pounds exactly. Fantastic, I thought, who cares about the food, I was catching.

Later that evening Vic and I decided to send some postcards back home and on our cards we both described how terrible the food was and how, after dinner, we were sneaking out at night to go into the village to get some fish and chips. Strangely enough, from the next day onwards there was a sudden marked improvement in the food, but we just couldn't understand why. Apart from all this, the fishing continued to be good and the following day I caught an 11 pound common whilst stalking and another double on the last day. Unfortunately for Vic, no carp came his way during the week but I knew he thoroughly enjoyed the session as much as I did.

It was not until we were on our way home that it dawned on me why the food had suddenly improved. After breakfast one morning we walked down the road to post our postcards and the proprietor just happened to be going our way too. He kindly offered to post them for us and without thinking we said "Yes". He obviously read them!

Memories of Waterways will always remain clear in my mind for it was the first real carp water that I fished and in those days, unlike now, it took an angler several years to become proficient at carp fishing. I like to think of it as the water on which I served my 'apprenticeship' for five years, learning slowly from my own mistakes with little help from others. How things have changed today! However, it would be nice to finish this chapter with the story of my first twenty and I am pleased to say that it was in fact one of the Waterways beauties.

It was during my fourth season on the water and I was fishing the Boat House swim. The one thing that remains clear in my mind is the fight that this fish gave me and even today, having caught more than 150 fish over 20 pounds, I still believe that this fish fought as powerfully as any other carp I have played. The fight lasted about 45 minutes and at first the big fish made several powerful dashes to the large lily bed which grew on a shallow mound of gravel in the centre of the lake. I remember turning it just inches from the pads only to have it make more heart-pounding runs to the same sanctuary. But it wasn't so much that part of the fight that impressed me so much, it was the dogged, very powerful lunges at close range that I couldn't believe. For at least 30 minutes the fish moved slowly, backwards and forwards hugging the bottom and no matter how hard I tried I could not lift its head. As time went on I remember thinking to myself that this 'thing' must be something else. I had not experienced anything so powerful and my whole body was aching. I called across to my friend in the poor light and I said, "This can't be a carp, there's no way it's a carp. It must be a catfish, it's fighting like a man". Why I thought it was a catfish I just don't know because I'd never caught one or seen one, but I had read of their incredible fighting qualities. However, my painful enjoyment eventually abated when I managed to pull the leviathan over the waiting net carefully offered by my friend. Like two young kids we excitedly carried the fish up the bank where we discovered, to my surprise, that it was a carp, a mirror weighing $22\frac{1}{4}$ pounds — my first twenty.

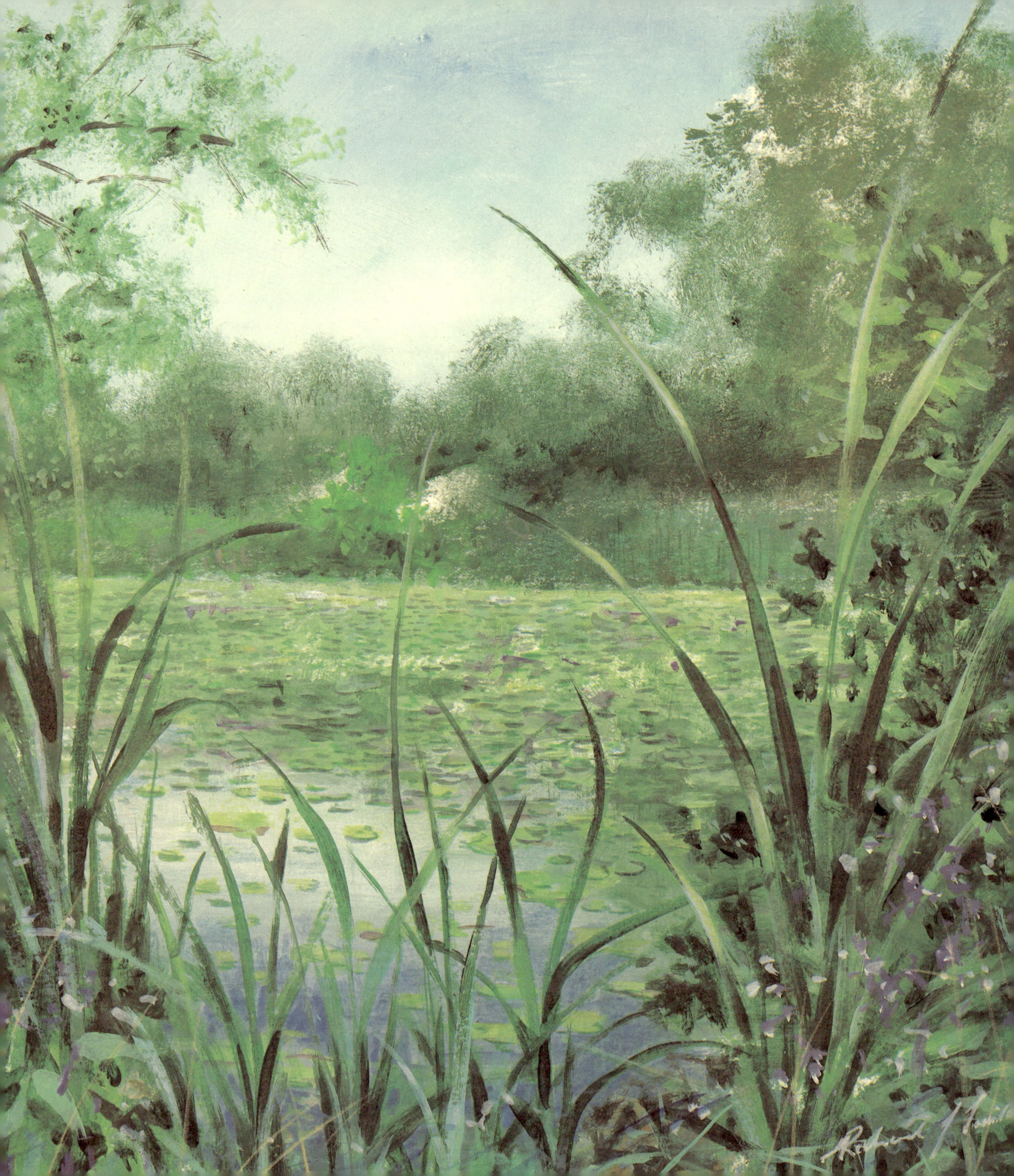

Ashlea Pool

I joined the BCSG in 1976 but I might well have been a member sooner had I not been one of those who believed, quite mistakenly, that you needed to have caught a thirty to get in. In October '76 I did get my first '30', so I immediately applied for BCSG membership. I had wanted to apply a year before, but it was not until I met Tony Harrison at Waterways that I realised I had a good chance of getting in. I was accepted, and joining the BCSG is one of the best things I have ever done — not only because I was then able to get my name on the waiting list for Ashlea Pool, which at the time was kept by Peter Mohan for BCSG members only, but for many other reasons in connection with the people I met through the Group, the magazines I was then able to read and the meetings I was able to go to.

At that time there were very few waters in the country which held really big carp; in fact, you could count those that did on the fingers of two hands. For this reason, it meant very much more than it does today to be able to get into a really big fish water. Today there are literally dozens of waters of this kind; then there were very few — and Ashlea Pool was one of the few. Once my name was on the waiting list and I knew that there was a good chance I would get in I spent a lot of time trying to find out about the lake. I thought about it a lot too and got hold of all the old records and read everything about the water which I could lay my hands on. Nowadays, the situation has changed, and with so many big fish waters about we tend to have a more casual attitude about them.

I was fortunate enough to be offered Ashlea membership the following year, in 1977, and my first impressions of the place are most important. Unlike Peter Mohan, who told me that his first impression was of a water so small that he felt there couldn't possibly be really big fish in it, my first thoughts were of the huge masses of weed which covered the water to the extent that there was literally no open water. How could anyone get a big fish out of a lake like that, I remember thinking. In fact, it was the weed problem which beat a lot of good carp anglers who joined Ashlea, most of whom left without ever catching a fish. Their confidence was so sapped by seeing the weed that they never recovered, and it is largely for this reason that they failed at the water. Although I felt as intimidated by the weed as many of the others, I try to think logically, and I made myself remember that other anglers had succeeded in taking big carp from the water, so if they could do so, I could do it too. However, I must admit that I tended to avoid the weed on my first few trips, and I spent much of the time fishing the open deeper water bay which had been dug out the previous year by the owner, when the level in the main lake had gone so low that the big fish had their backs out of the water.

For those who have never seen Ashlea, I had better explain that it is an old railway ballast pit — a type of gravel pit, really — of about $1\frac{1}{4}$ acres in size. I was impressed by the crystal clear water, but was amazed to find that although half of the lake only was covered with lily pads, even in the apparently clear areas the bottom of the lake was invisible, as huge 'cabbages' and other weed completely covered the whole area of the lake. Often no fish could be seen; they were obviously moving beneath the green carpet of weed which covered the bottom. In addition, I was surprised to find that there was not a lot of cover round much of the lake, although there were a number of low bushes mainly on the side where the hides had been built, and there were, fortunately, some good climbing trees, which I like.

It was bitterly cold on my first session in late June, and I only stayed for 27 hours. I found three fish, a common and two very big mirrors, in a hole in the weed, and they stayed there the whole time without moving; they showed no interest in any baits, so I set up in swim No.14, at the point of the deep, clear bay. (See diagram) My second trip lasted the same length of time, but I fished hide number two, which is on the opposite side from the bay. The hides had been constructed of wood and grassed over, but I soon realised that they only gave cover from the rain and wind; they were open at the front, and so low that they were very awkward to fish from. They were not in good fish-catching areas anyway, and I soon made up my mind that I would not fish them again. I'm sure that the carp soon came to know that someone was at the hides, and that they avoided that part of the lake for this reason. There was a small cleared channel early in the season opposite the hides, but the fish rarely fed in the small amount of clear water which was there and by mid-summer this channel became overgrown with lilies.

Although the Ashlea rota allowed you to go every other week — on your week off you were not allowed there at all — I didn't get back until late September. On arrival I saw a fish swim out of the open bay, and another actually rolled in the bay, which was very unusual. Since I still wanted to avoid the weed

ASHLEA POOL

anyway this really appealed to me, and I set up three rods in swim No. 14. One bait was placed in the entrance to the bay, one further out, and the left hand rod was cast to the only clump of lilies about four feet out from the bank. Bait on this rod was a suspended Yestamin boily fished about 18 inches from the bottom amongst the small patch of lilies. I started at mid-day and nothing happened until 8.10am the following morning, when I had a two inch twitch on the left hand rod. This alerted me and ten minutes later the indicator went up and I struck into my first Ashlea carp. I just managed to keep it out of the lilies in the main lake and then I soon landed it from the very awkward shaped bank. The fish weighed 27lbs 2ozs., and was later identified as one of the few original fish left in the lake, a lovely fish known as 'Scarface' and one which I found dead in the following year.

In mid-October I fished my fourth and last session of the season without any result, although I stayed there for 47 hours.

Readers might be surprised that I fished Ashlea so comparatively little during this first season, but my fishing was going very well on other waters, and I had 21 twenties that season altogether — which was remarkable for the days before the coming of the hair rig.

I managed seven sessions the following year in 1978, a total of 300 hours at the water. Only two of these sessions are perhaps worth mentioning, and on the fourth trip I decided on a different approach. I scattered considerable quantities of Felix Meaty Crunch, a cat food floater, about the lake, and on the first day found two fish taking very cautiously. Eventually, one took the hook bait, but I didn't strike as the line failed to move. The fish then ejected the bait and bolted.

I often took 20 boxes of cat food floaters with me, and put in the contents of around six boxes straight away. If there are 500 pieces in each box this means that I put in around, 10,000 floaters! One of the reasons for doing this was to beat the ducks, which competed with the carp for the floaters until they got full up. The ducks could actually be seen pecking at the backs of the carp to drive them away. Since it was essential to use only one floater because the fish were extremely wary, I used a large hook, a size 2 Lion D'or and balanced this by putting a piece of polystyrene in the hole in the centre of the Felix Meaty Crunch. I used a home-made self-cocking quill on the line as a casting weight, and this was attached at the bottom by a float ring. The quill was about 12 inches from the hook; it had to be as near as this because of the lily pads. Since carp often 'mouth' the floaters the bait is not always in the mouth even when it disappears, and I found it best to watch the float rather than the bait when using this method.

    On the second day I did the same, and found two fish, 'Humpy', a thirty, and 'Kinky' at about 20, feeding on the floater. Kinky eventually took the hook bait, and remembering what had happened on the previous day, I struck at once. This was in a very heavily weeded area, but fortunately I was using one of my $2\frac{1}{4}$lb test curve carbon rods, and this rod has such a positive action that I was able to haul into the fish and keep it on the surface, which beat the weed. The line was 12lb. breaking strain. After a short fight I landed the fish which weighed 21lb 14ozs.

Our rota had now taken five fish, four of them recently, and the other rota had virtually given up, so between our visits the water was quite often getting a full week's rest. If only we could catch another fish it would conclude a golden and unprecedented season for Ashlea, I thought. My usual preliminary mind-racking thoughts had again put the emphasis on stalking the fish, instead of my old ways of having a quick look around, picking a fancied swim and sitting in it hiding for two or three days. I had wasted most of my time the previous season and even a little time this season at Ashlea fishing with this completely wrong approach. I don't know what made me fish that way but I suppose it was the combination of several things. Firstly, I was into the habit of fishing the whole session in one swim and never leaving the rods, for stalking the fish was virtually impossible on my other waters. I had then read Jack Hilton's book which seemed to emphasise this approach which was further confirmed by the owner who told me of how Jack would never come out of a swim for days. I was then told by others that once you showed yourself to the fish you'd had it for a week.

All this had misled me into fishing Ashlea badly and only Geoff Booth's stalking results made me reconsider my approach. Until this time Geoff had certainly been the most successful Ashlea angler ever and his approach had to be seen to be appreciated. It may be true that Geoff spent a lot of time at Ashlea, but he did spend it catching fish whereas many other good anglers also spent a lot of time there not catching fish! So, with all this in mind I arrived at the pool determined not to start until I had found some fish. As I walked along the field side it became obvious that unless the fish were active I would not find them as the light was poor and a westerly wind together with light rain was rippling the surface. Despite this I found some fish in a hole amongst the cabbages on the wood side at the deep end of the pool. The following two hours were spent holding a rod, kneeling down in the rain until I was aching all over and soaked right through. During this time there were at least three fish in the hole all the time and occasionally there were five. I could only make out dark shapes even though one of these was probably one of two big fish I had never seen before. Frequently the fish seemed to inspect the bait but there was no movement of the line and eventually the fish moved out. As soon as they had moved out I quickly climbed a nearby tree and I could see that two large fish had gone over to the other side of the pool whereas the others had disappeared. I then walked back round to the other side and climbed a tree where I had last seen the fish. Watching from the top of the tree I could see the two big fish moving between two holes in the weed. They were spending about a minute swimming around inside one hole and then lifting up over the cabbages which grow to within about 2½' of the surface, going to the other hole and doing the same. I watched these fish for about fifteen minutes continually moving from one hole to the other. I then worked out exactly where the holes were as they could not be seen from the pitch below, and I had never fished the swim, No. 18, before. One hole was halfway across the pool about four feet out from an ash tree on the private house bank, and the other hole was a quarter of the way across in a direct line with the third hide on the wood side. After bearing all that in mind, I quickly set up two rods with very sensitive link-ledger rigs. I grabbed the two different mixes of paste bait I had in the car and hastily moulded a small piece onto the first rod leaving some of the large hook exposed. I then made a cast to the hole furthest out which seemed to land a little too near the ash tree, so I reeled in and re-cast, this time into the exact spot I wanted. I clipped the bobbin onto the line and put the line round the buzzer antenna. I then opened the bail arm as a temporary measure whilst I baited the other rod but as I picked up the other rod the buzzer sounded, and the bobbin rose quickly to the butt ring.

 I immediately struck hard and was into a fish. For the first few seconds I was not in control of the fish for it was kiting at an angle towards me and the house bank to my right. The rod was bent double but with little sustained pressure on the fish. By the time I had recovered some line the fish had an overhanging branch of another ash tree between us. At first this didn't worry me as the line was clear of the branch and I thought the fish would come away from the bank as I gained line. Unfortunately, this didn't happen, for as I gained line I couldn't turn the fish with sidestrain from the rod and I just simply pulled it towards the branch which was half in the water. The fight then became a stalemate as the line got caught over the branch.

 Several times I let the fish gain line only to bring it back to the branch again. After a while of this the fish was beaten and lay on the surface amongst the growth of the branch. For what seemed like ages I couldn't make my mind up what to do, for I had never been in for a fish before and didn't particularly want to go in for this one. It's not the water I was frightened of, it's just that I've never thought a capture is 100% angling skill unless the fish is netted from the bank.

Eventually I decided I had no choice, for whatever I tried I just couldn't get the line off the branch, even though it was running freely over the top of it. After making certain the fish was lying on the surface I pushed the butt of the rod a couple of inches into the ground, and propped it up against the bushes which were at the side of the swim. I then wound down on the fish so that the rod was bent, and slackened off the clutch considerably, in case the fish decided to take off again. After a quick strip I waded out with the landing net, but to my surprise was out of my depth before I could reach the fish.

At this stage I was doubtful about carrying on, but after stopping for a few seconds I decided to get on with it, so I swam out to the fish. As I got to the fish it took a certain dislike to me being in the water with it and decided to throw a fit during which it pulled some line off the clutch. I then got hold of the line and gradually pulled it back onto the surface, which didn't prove that easy an operation as I was treading water and holding the line and fish with the other hand. The fish went into the net whereupon it went berserk, leaping out of the net and swimming a complete circle around me pulling the line tight around my waist!

At this stage I was completely fed up with the whole operation and wished I hadn't gone in. To cut a long story short I managed to get loose and when I got the fish into the net again I snapped off one of the fibre glass landing net arms, bit through the line and came ashore on the house bank with the owner laughing at me in my undies. He shouted for his wife to get the camera, but I was quick enough to avoid the embarrassment.

The fish turned out to be 'Humpy', and weighed 33lb 2oz. I made a decision then and there that the next time I go in for a fish it will either have to be at least an upper thirty or have its life in danger.

That fish happened to be the last one taken during the year even though I visited the pool once more and Geoff and Alan fished another five weekends up to the end of November.

There can be no disputing that 1978 was a golden year for Ashlea. 'Super Rota' had taken six fish and considering the amount of fish the pool now held it must surely have been the best-ever season.

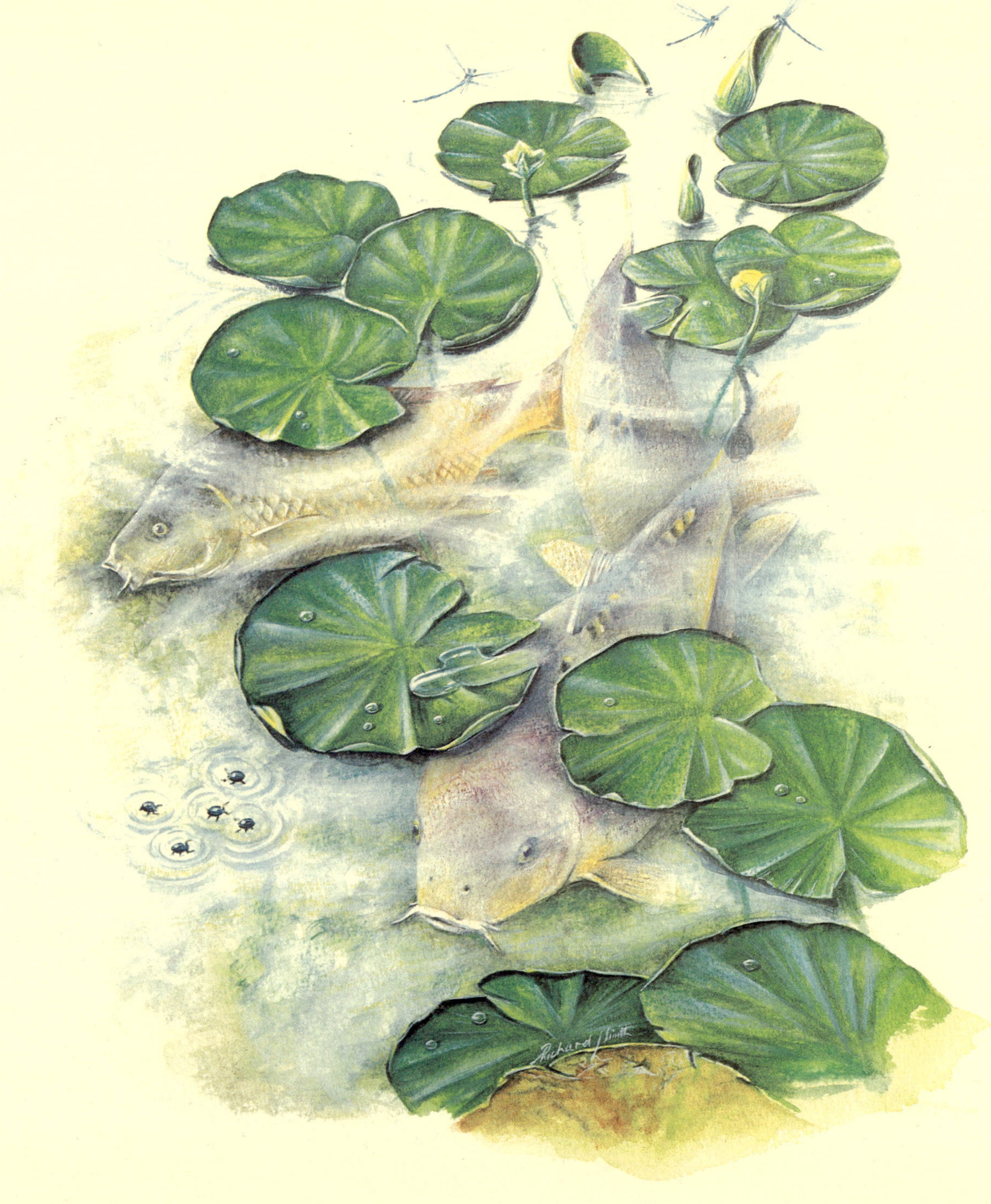

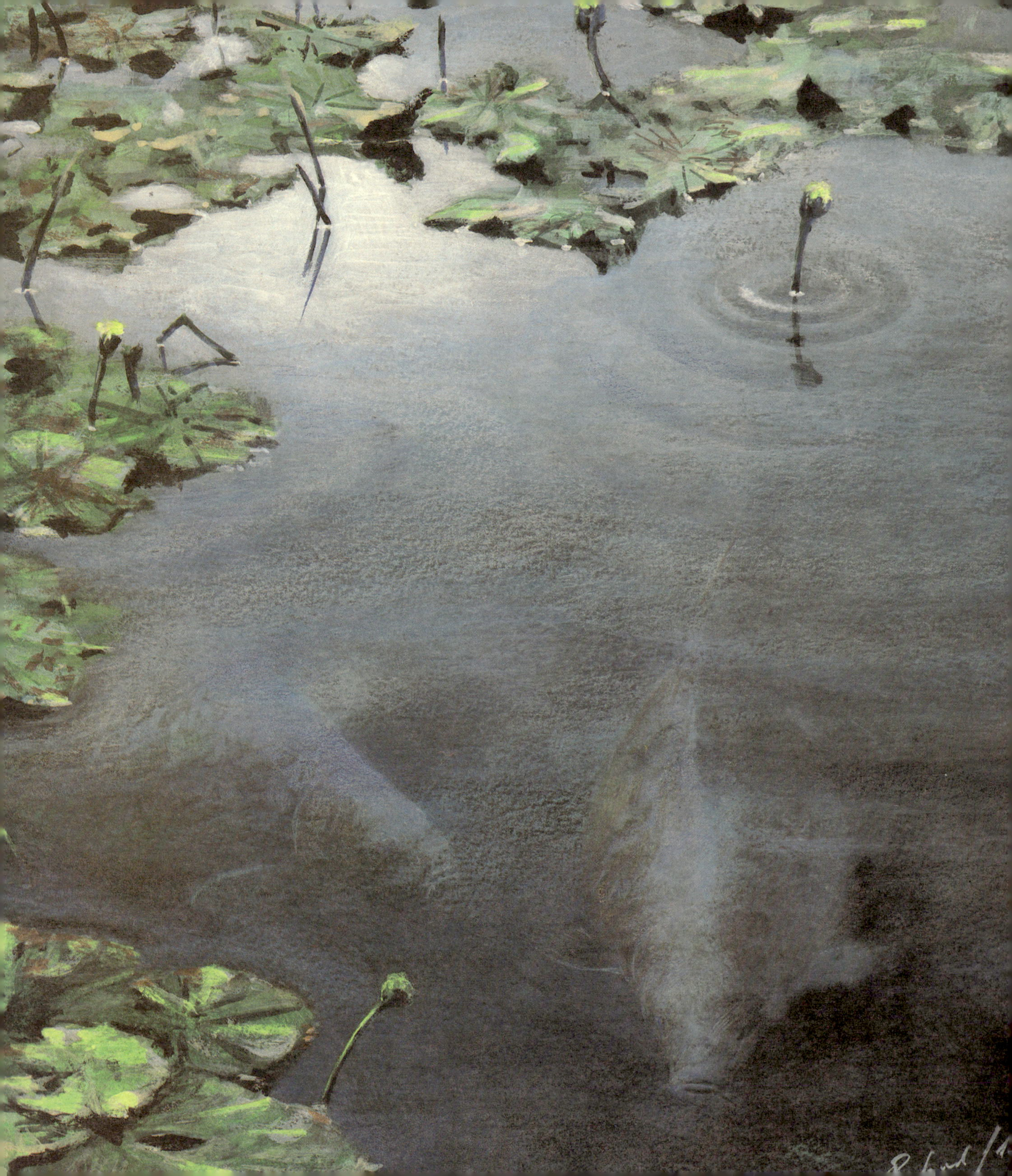

STRANGE ENCOUNTERS...

In fifteen years of carp fishing, many amusing and strange incidents have occurred; most of these were funny, and some even frightening at the time, although they may not seem as dramatic in writing. What appeared funny at the time — to me — may not make the reader of this book laugh at all, but all the stories in this chapter are true, and I can only hope you find them interesting.

Some years ago I was fishing Longfield, at Staines, with Ron Middleton. It was shortly after dark, when I suddenly heard a really loud scraping noise in my left ear — in fact, it seemed right inside my head. In addition to this I could feel a strange wriggling movement which was frightening to say the least — I had never experienced anything like it. In a panic, I rushed round the lake to Ron to see if he could see anything in my ear using his torch. I kept shouting "Can't you hear anything, can't you hear anything?" For ages he put his ear against mine: good thing we weren't observed! The noise was so loud to me that I couldn't understand it when he kept saying "No". By this time I was really panicking and I told him that if he couldn't find anything in 30 seconds, I was going to rush off to the nearest hospital.

At last, after what seemed an eternity, he said he could see it and started to laugh. "What is it, what is it?" I said, but his laughter turned to hysterics and so much so that he couldn't speak. As you imagine, this did little to alleviate my trauma and I was beginning to throw a fit! Ron, being an intelligent fella, could see that I was about to commit hari-kari and shouted "It's an elephant." Then it crawled out on its own — it was merely an ant!

At first light the following morning a carp angler from the other side of the lake appeared and enquired as to what had caused such a bitter argument between my friend and I. "An ant", I said. He gave me such a look and obviously thought I was quite mad because to this day he has never spoken a word to me.

The next incident occurred at Ashlea, where I was fishing with a friend. We soon spotted swirls from under a bush, and my friend said he would have a go for the fish, although it wasn't visible. Over the next five hours, employing great stealth and making careful use of the light breeze, he drifted free offerings under the bush — ripples appeared and the baits were always taken. After a short while he figured that the fish was taking confidently but each time his floater went under the bush and was taken, he struck — and missed. Eventually, I went along to see what had happened; he still hadn't seen the fish, so with his permission I crept cautiously down to see if I could see what took his next floater. I was in a very awkward position and found it difficult to lean out far enough to see clearly underneath. I watched his bait drift into the margins and when it was almost out of sight some ripples appeared and I saw the 'fish'. It had a pointed nose and several whiskers — I can't repeat here what my mate said when I informed him that for five hours he'd been feeding a large rat!

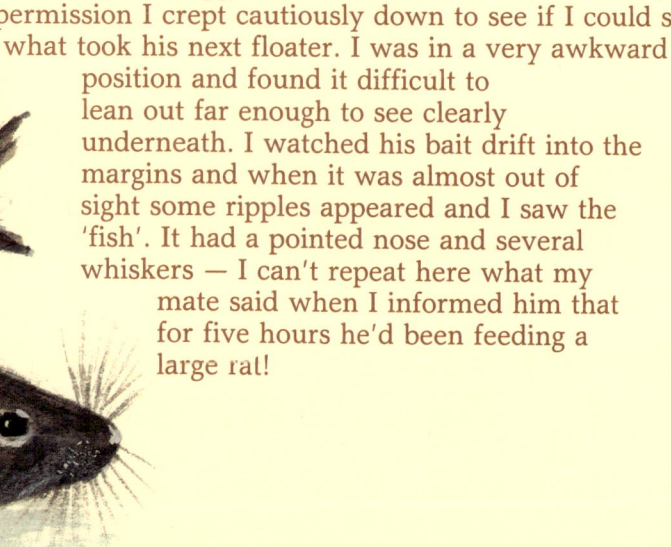

As most carp anglers know, Calor Gas can be dangerous and I once nearly found this out the hard way. I was using my gas stove to boil some water at Marlborough Pool, Oxford one very cold winter's day. The gas was running out and I couldn't get the kettle to boil. I thought a good idea to thaw it out was to put the gas bottle on its own ring, to which it is connected by a flexible pipe. I know this should never be done but I quite often found it necessary. The trouble was, I forgot it when I had a run and hooked a fish. Standing in front of the gas bottle, I played the fish but couldn't understand why I was getting hotter and hotter. At last it dawned on me and I looked round to see the gas bottle enveloped in a huge sheet of flame; it was about to explode. I wasn't going to risk losing the fish, so I kept kicking out at the gas bottle, and at last I kicked it off the ring. After landing the fish I managed to turn the gas off, but the bottle was red hot. I've not made that mistake again, I can tell you.

Anyone who has fished Lockwood Reservoir knows just how far you have to walk; it's about two miles round. Whilst walking round with a companion one day I smelt a strong burning smell and we both remarked about it every couple of hundred yards or so. I didn't think much of this at first, as there are many strange smells in that area. Eventually I saw smoke coming from the bottom of my friend's trouser legs — and he seemed quite unaware of anything amiss. His jeans were smouldering like mad and I began to laugh. He then realised what was happening — he was on fire. Without hesitation he screamed and leapt straight into ten feet of water — that put the fire out! The strange thing was that we never found out how his trousers had caught on fire and to this day I still can't imagine how it happened.

I have never liked fishing on wet wooden platforms and for this I have a good reason. One night at Marlborough I was fishing on a very slippery platform, which I could just about wade out to. In the middle of the night I was dozing on the bed chair, when I suddenly felt something moving — it was my bed chair, sliding across the platform, and launching me into the water, still in my sleeping bags. This was in January, and it was bitterly cold. All my gear went in with me as well, including my rods, buzzers, kit bag and brolly! This was the only time I ever had to pack up and go home part way through a session, but I was back four hours later!

'G' Lake at Waveney Valley used to be overrun with rats which ate their way into your tackle bags, ran over your legs and were a great nuisance; they are no doubt still there. We decided to take along some rat traps, but no matter how hard we tried we couldn't catch them in the traps. Three or four hours were spent setting the traps in various places and positions. We even dug then into the ground so that nothing was visible except the bait but still they managed to take the bait and escape. As a last resort we decided to angle for them. We used a spool of line and attached a hook (barbless of course) and a bait, but even this failed. We then set-up a rod along the bank besides the path and 'fished' for them properly, but they simply wouldn't get hooked even with advanced 'bolt' and 'hair' rigs. We had dozens of runs and we tried all night, but failed. The rats disappeared at dawn and we were completely worn out. In addition to this I had a huge swollen thumb, caused by setting the traps too light, and we were ratless!

When I was a young boy and ignorant, I knew nothing about permits and close seasons, and one day I went with daredevil John, the Lincolnshire poacher, to try to catch some small carp for my tank. We started on this lake at about midnight — John had a key to the gate which he obtained from an ex-member. Unusually, this square lake was completely surrounded by a 6 foot wire fence, and inside the fence all around the lake was only about six feet of bank before you came to a sheer drop into the water.

John took me to the 'hot spot' — I had never been to the water before — and we set-up and started to fish. Within half an hour John had caught two small commons, which we put into a sack. We carried on, as we needed a third fish, but after a while we thought we saw car headlights through the undergrowth, coming down the lane. Then we heard, to our horror, the noise of the chain on the gate being opened. Since we had left our car in front of the gate we knew they were on to us — or someone was.

Whoever was there couldn't be more than 25 yards away, so we started to pack up with great rapidity. Having more to lose than John I was ready first, but by then I could see the light of a torch on the path, coming towards us. I panicked and bolted, crashing along the narrow and unfamiliar path in the dark and leaving John behind.

Eventually, I got to a corner, and turned right, climbing over a tree across the path, thinking to myself that the bailiffs were bound to catch me — they knew the place and I didn't. Just then, I saw a big open lorry in a yard beyond the fence. Quickly, I slung my tackle over the fence, and in a few seconds I was up and into the back of the lorry, where I hid. I was certain I had been seen. Peering over the edge of the lorry I saw the torches coming, but to my amazement, there was no John — I had assumed that he was behind me, but he wasn't and I had passed no exit on the way.

I was equally surprised when the two torch-carrying bailiffs dashed past and went on down the bank — they hadn't seen me after all.

They disappeared, and I stayed in the lorry for what seemed like an age, though it can't have been more than half an hour — the trouble was I wasn't sure where the bailiffs were. At last I climbed out of the lorry, and leaving my tackle behind I started to try to find my way back to the entrance via an adjoining lake — not easy in the dark — when you don't know the place. I daren't call out for John in case the bailiffs were still there and heard me — and it was his car anyway so I couldn't get home without him.

I kept searching, but it was not until 4am that I got back to the car — and saw someone standing by it. It was John, at last, and of course he had been searching, in silence, for me. He told me that he had escaped by slinging his gear into the water, pulling his Barbour over his head and lying down against the fence — and the bailiffs went by without seeing him — inches from his head. There was a note on the windscreen from the bailiffs saying they had got our number — and John's father, from whom he had borrowed the car, was a policeman!

We went home and fortunately heard no more.

I don't make a habit of poaching — especially these days but I do have another poaching story, which occurred on a large no-night fishing club water. I was always nervous when fishing without permission, and had given myself a crick in the neck looking round for anyone official. Suddenly I saw a figure walking along the bank, silhouetted in the moonlight. I tried to hide my gear in a small patch of rushes, and I crouched down near the water, but without much hope, as this is one of the most open lakes in the country. I kept crouched by the water, motionless, hoping I wasn't seen, but the footsteps came closer in the darkness, and then all of a sudden someone tapped me on the shoulder. I jumped about a foot in the air, turned round, and was most relieved to find it was Terrible Tony — a fellow poacher.

In my early days of carp fishing I used to fish Waterways, often by the boathouse. On one very hot day in 1976, I suddenly heard a tremendous crash to my right in some marginal rushes. Then there was a great splashing in the water and about half a minute later in front of me a bald head surfaced — it was the owner of the water — swimming! I always thought water owners were potty.

"Come on in", he called in his posh voice, "it's lovely and warm". What could I say — if you own the place, you can do as you please — even if you do ruin the swim.

Lots of things happened at Ashlea — I can remember one or two. On one occasion I was asleep on the bank without a brolly in swim No. 18, and I awoke feeling a strange hot puff of breath on my face — and found I was looking straight up the nostrils of a horse, about three inches from my face. It took me a few seconds in the dark to work out what the nostrils and big thick tongue belonged to, and I expect the horse was equally startled!

On another dark night at Ashlea in one of my first sessions I was fishing in No. 3 hide which has an entrance at the back, which you had to crawl through to get into the hide. This was covered by a corrugated tin sheet to stop the rain pouring in. I was lying back on my bedchair within the pitch blackness of the hide, with my head not more than two feet from the tin, when all of a sudden it started to move. I was transfixed with horror — I simply couldn't move. The tin started crashing and banging above me, and I was convinced that some very large creature was about to fall on me, in the middle of the night.

Eventually, I forced myself to leap off the bedchair, grab my torch and crawl out at the front of the hide; in the light of the beam I saw the hind quarters of a huge badger disappearing into the undegrowth!

I suppose a good way to end this section of the book would be a story against myself!

I have already said that when I was young I occasionally

broke the rules — and not many people can honestly say that they did not! On this occasion, I was fishing alone on a lonely lake where I had no right to be at night, with my car parked partly obscured by some trees about 50 yards away, and above me, as the path from the lake sloped steeply upward.

Just as I was packing up, I thought I heard a noise by the car, and I shone a torch towards it — and a torch flashed back! Gathering my remaining tackle up, I almost leapt along a path which went away from the car, and wound along the precipitous side of the lake next door. After a few yards and out of sight of the car, I stopped and listened. There was silence — whoever it was, was not following me — he must be waiting by the car to catch me — or so said my guilty conscience.

To cut a long story short, it took me half an hour to approach the car by a roundabout route, creeping along in the dark with all my tackle, round one of the, wildest, loneliest, spookiest lakes in England. Within sight of the car at last, I hid my tackle and literally crept, on my stomach, to where I could see the car. There was no-one there. I lay still for another quarter of an hour until I was certain the place was deserted, then tip-toed to the car. Still no-one. Why had they left? I peered down towards the black lake where I had been fishing — and then it struck me, so I hurried down to the swim — and flashed the torch towards the car. There was a return flash; not another torch, but a reflection from my car window!

A guilty conscience makes cowards of us all!

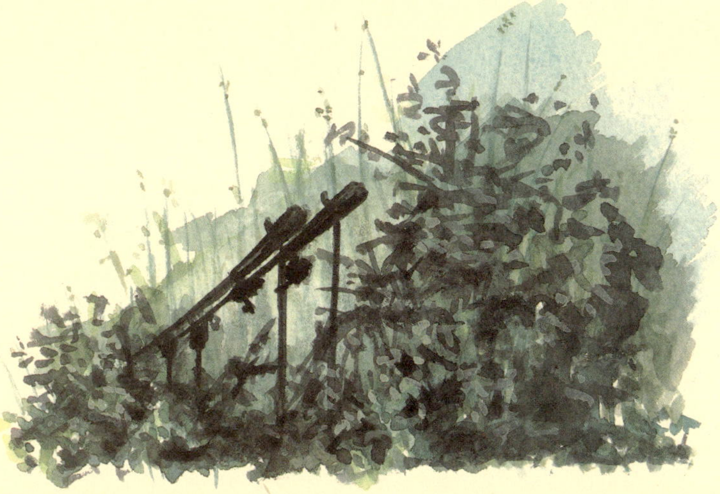

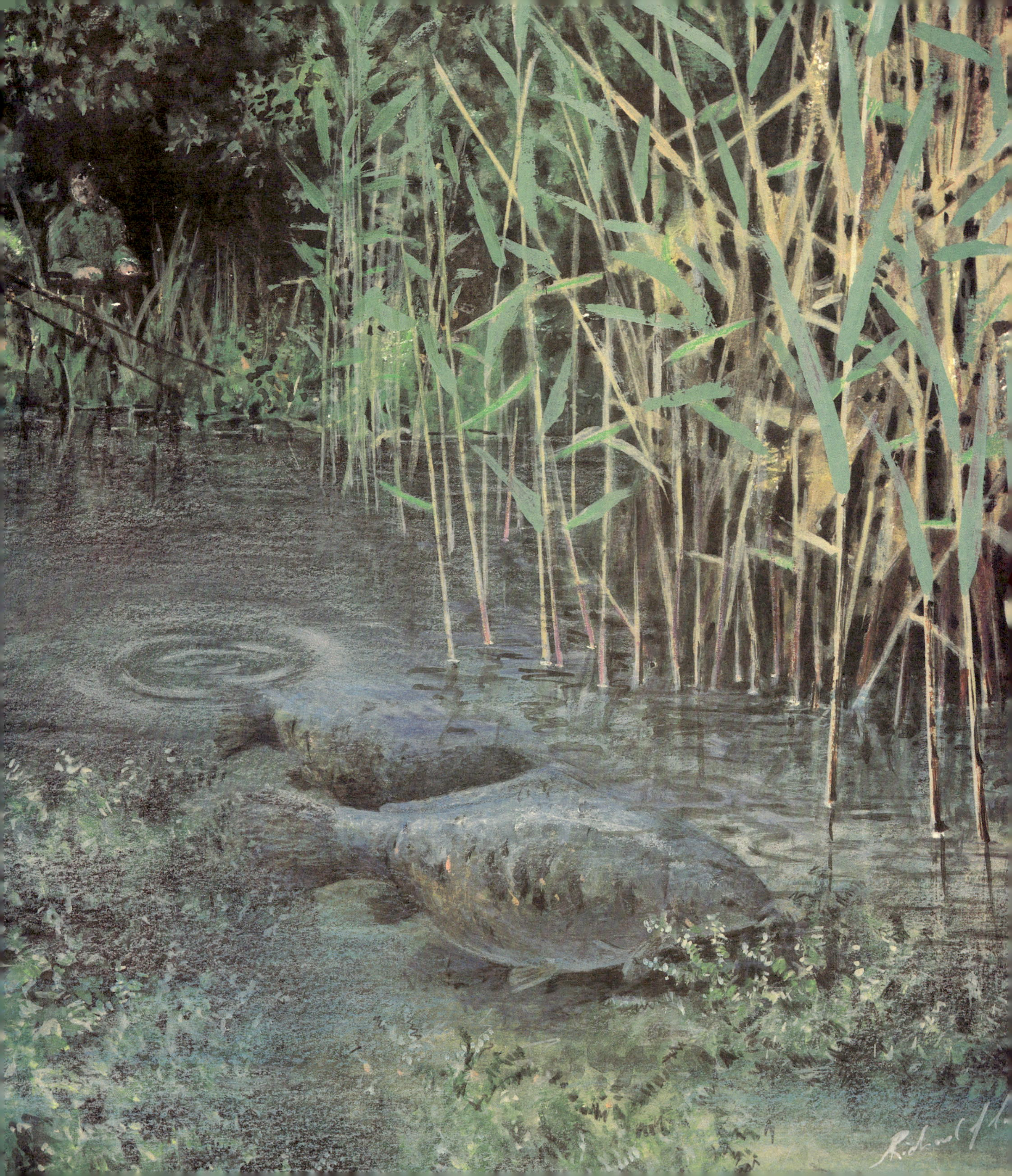

Redmire

Although it seems to be most carp anglers dream to fish Redmire Pool, to me it turned out to be just another carp water. I was not in any way affected by the nostalgia and history of the place, although I respected it as a good carp water, and went there determined to keep to the rules and to work hard to succeed.

Since many anglers had been there and caught so little, I had been given the impression that it was very hard. I didn't find it so as I caught 23 twenties including two thirties in my first and only season there. Why did so many anglers fail? This I cannot understand, because Redmire is so heavily stocked that it must be an easy water — if the rules had allowed me to go every week I think I could have had more than 50 twenties in the season.

There were so many fish that line bites were constant, and takes were so frequent that I found the water to be much less interesting than Ashlea, which is a fascinating water to fish.

Redmire was just a sort of 20's factory, so much so that I used it for bait and rig experiments. I'm sorry if this upsets those who would like to regard Redmire as a superwater, with super hard fish, but I am simply relating the facts as I found them. However, in this chapter I will avoid relating the hard facts on baits, rigs and catches as these can be found in my chapter in that marvellous book *Redmire Pool* where my diary facts are repeated verbatim.

Memories of the water? I have plenty. On one occasion I saw some early morning fish bubbling off the In-Willow swim. I had tiger nuts with me for the first time, so I heavily baited the area that evening. It was a very quiet, calm night interrupted only by the hooting of an owl but when I woke up in the morning I saw the most extraordinary sight. More than one third of the lake was covered with bubbles, all of which were emanating from my swim; the carp had not only found the nuts, but were feeding on them with abandon.

You can imagine how I felt; what could induce more confidence than a sight like this — I couldn't fail to catch. I had three twenties to 29.13 and unfortunately lost two others, neither of which were my fault. In fact I could well have missed out on the biggest fish had I not refused to have a cup of tea with the other two members of my rota for I caught the big mirror whilst they were in the hut drinking theirs. Normally I wouldn't miss a cup of 'liquid gold' for anything but this time that sixth sense told me not to leave the rods. The 29.13 was a beautiful fish; it had not been caught very often but I was fortunate enough to land it twice and strangely enough on both occasions it took the bait the second it hit the bottom. The first time was casting from the Evening Swim across to the opposite margins using a cream boilie; the reel churned backwards before I could open the bale arm and put the indicator on. On the second occasion I had just re-cast a tiger nut and the fish took it as I was fixing the indicator.

On another day I remember climbing a tree by the In-Willow swim and watching some big fish through my polaroids. I walked along a branch over the water, leant out holding on by one hand, when suddenly it snapped. I was precipitated head first into two feet of water and three feet of silt, from the very top of the tree, over 30 feet up! The branches I hit on the way down really hurt, and left me with many bruises. It caused quite a laugh when I crawled out of the lake covered from head to feet in stinking black silt. I later managed to fish out my polaroids with the landing net and about a fortnight later the story was reported in *Angling Times:* I wonder who put that in, and why?

One of the fish I always particularly wanted to catch was a beautiful common that had been caught by another member. One day I was creeping about in the shallows when I saw this fish circling some tree roots, along with a smaller common. With great caution I got nearer, swung out a cream boilie, and within 30 seconds had a take. Hoping it was the one I wanted, I played it hard and it fought like the devil, causing great bow waves in the very shallow water, but of course it was the smaller fish at 15lbs. Fortunately a large single tiger nut caught it eventually later in September, and it weighed 27lbs 14ozs. Without a doubt, this was the best looking fish in the lake.

I was always of the opinion that Redmire fish could be caught on any bait and on one session when I had already caught twenties on both boilies and tiger nuts I had some maple flavoured peanuts with me as well.

I climbed a tree in the Evening Swim and saw some fish coming in very close to the bank. From the tree I dropped in some of the peanuts, and as usual as the Redmire fish did with almost any bait you threw at them, they immediately went down and started to feed on them. I hastily climbed down, set up a rod with a peanut on it and cast it in, propping the rod against the tree, with the bail arm open. As I was in an impatient mood, I started to climb the tree again. By the time I was half way up the tree I spotted a good fish coming towards the bait and by the time I'd reached the top the fish took it. It seemed to take an age to get down, with line pouring from the spool, but eventually I succeeded, and landed a 22.12 common — a nice way to round off a five fish catch — and the session then came to an end because the owner of the lake 'asked our permission' for some children to go out in the boat — we could hardly refuse!

All waters seem to contain one exceptionally hard fighting fish and some that just 'give up' when hooked and Redmire is no exception. It was during the session I last mentioned when, at about 11pm, whilst fishing from Greenbanks that I hooked what appeared to be an eel. I was fishing only about two rod lengths out and at no time did the fish take an inch of line. A weird 'wriggling' sensation could be felt through the rod and on two occasions the fish went completely solid and the only way I could get it moving again was to heave back on the rod. I suppose in all the fish took no more than three minutes to land and it turned out to be a really nice looking linear mirror of $24\frac{1}{4}$ pounds. The area in front of me was completely clear of weed and contained no snags and I am still baffled as to how the fish became completely motionless and why such a good-sized fish, should not attempt to take line at such close range.

However, it was during the same session that I hooked Redmire's 'fighting fish'. Two nights before, at 2.20 in the morning I heard a fish roll twice over my baits. I sat up on my bedchair and before I could put the kettle on I had a steaming run on the middle rod. For about ten minutes there was no way I could even consider trying to get out of bed for the fish belted up and down at varying speeds, frequently changing direction. Normally, after about half a minute I find I can slip out of the sleeping bags but not with this fish. Half an hour later I was still playing the fish and my arm was aching so much so that for the first time ever I was forced to change over to my left arm for a short while. In all, it took me an hour to land the $23\frac{3}{4}$ pound fully scaled mirror and the next time it was caught by another syndicate member it took just as long.

Generally, I found the Redmire fish very easy to catch and much of my success could be put down to tree top observation. Several of the members never climbed trees, despite them being very easy to ascend, and I am certain that this is the main reason why catches were generally poor. By spending a little time up trees on every session you could not only very easily locate the main group of fish — you could see what depth they were feeding at (they were nearly always feeding every hour of the day somewhere in the pool) and how they were behaving. You could throw baits out to them, or cast lines amongst them and watch their reactions. It was then very easy to work out what methods would work. If you had this opportunity on all carp waters I am sure many of us would have given up carp fishing a long time ago — not being able to observe the habits of carp in most lakes is, I am sure, one of the main difficulties in carp fishing.

By observing the Redmire fish it soon became obvious that they avoided lines strewn across the swim. It could be seen that sunken lines frightened the fish less and so much of my fishing was done with very slack, sunken lines. This meant that on most occasions a fixed lead set up was required otherwise the fish could play around with the hook baits without you knowing. On one of my earlier sessions I had about ten twenties feeding very confidently on anything dropped down to them (this was not unusual; I often had up to twenty five twenties feeding confidently on free samples). I used these opportunities to test various set-ups, instead of being tempted to catch them and, as on this occasion, I often cast a baited rod amongst them set up as normal on the bank but with me up a tree. I watched several fish pick up the hook bait, which was fished on a standard free running link leger, and most of them moved at least a foot with the bait in their lips but no bite was registered on the buzzer despite the very short range being fished. It was not until one fish took the bait a distance of more than three feet that the slightest indication was noticed at the rod end — even then this fish dropped the bait before a single bleep was heard. This behaviour did not surprise me as I'd actually seen this happen on several other waters. It did, however, prove why most people failed to catch at Redmire — most anglers no doubt often had fish feeding on their baits but rarely did they get any indication on their ineffective rigs. A short time spent observing the fish would have saved thousands of wasted hours.

Another important factor was the amount of bait introduced. Again from overhead observation, it was obvious that on most occasions a small amount of bait was totally ignored and it was not until a decent amount was put in that one or two fish took notice. Once a fish was feeding on the baits others couldn't resist and soon joined in but great care was needed if you wanted to add bait whilst the fish were already present. They tolerated only very small amounts raining over their heads and the 'little and often' ploy was essential. Unless spooked, once feeding on the baits the Redmire carp did not stop until the area was totally cleared and because of this it was an advantage to bait heavily initially if no fish were present as the 'little and often' supply was not enough to keep up with the demand. Twenty 20's can eat an awful lot of food — much more than I'm prepared to introduce — so it was a matter of making the most of it whilst it lasted.

Really though, the Redmire fish behaved in a similar way to most other carp except for one exception. I shall never forget the first day I climbed one of the trees overlooking the shallow end of the pool. There, one could see huge craters amongst the silty bottom, most of them three to four feet deep. At first I wasn't sure what had caused them or whether they were permanent features but I soon found out the next time I had a look. Several carp could be seen vigorously rooting at a small spot on the bottom and they would remain feeding, totally pre-occupied, for perhaps eight hours until a huge crater had been excavated.

Gradually, over the course of about a week, the soft silt found its own level and these big holes disappeared soon to be replaced by new ones. I should imagine that these carp would have been very difficult to catch — I tried once and failed — but there were always other catchable fish feeding elsewhere in the pool so I never found out.

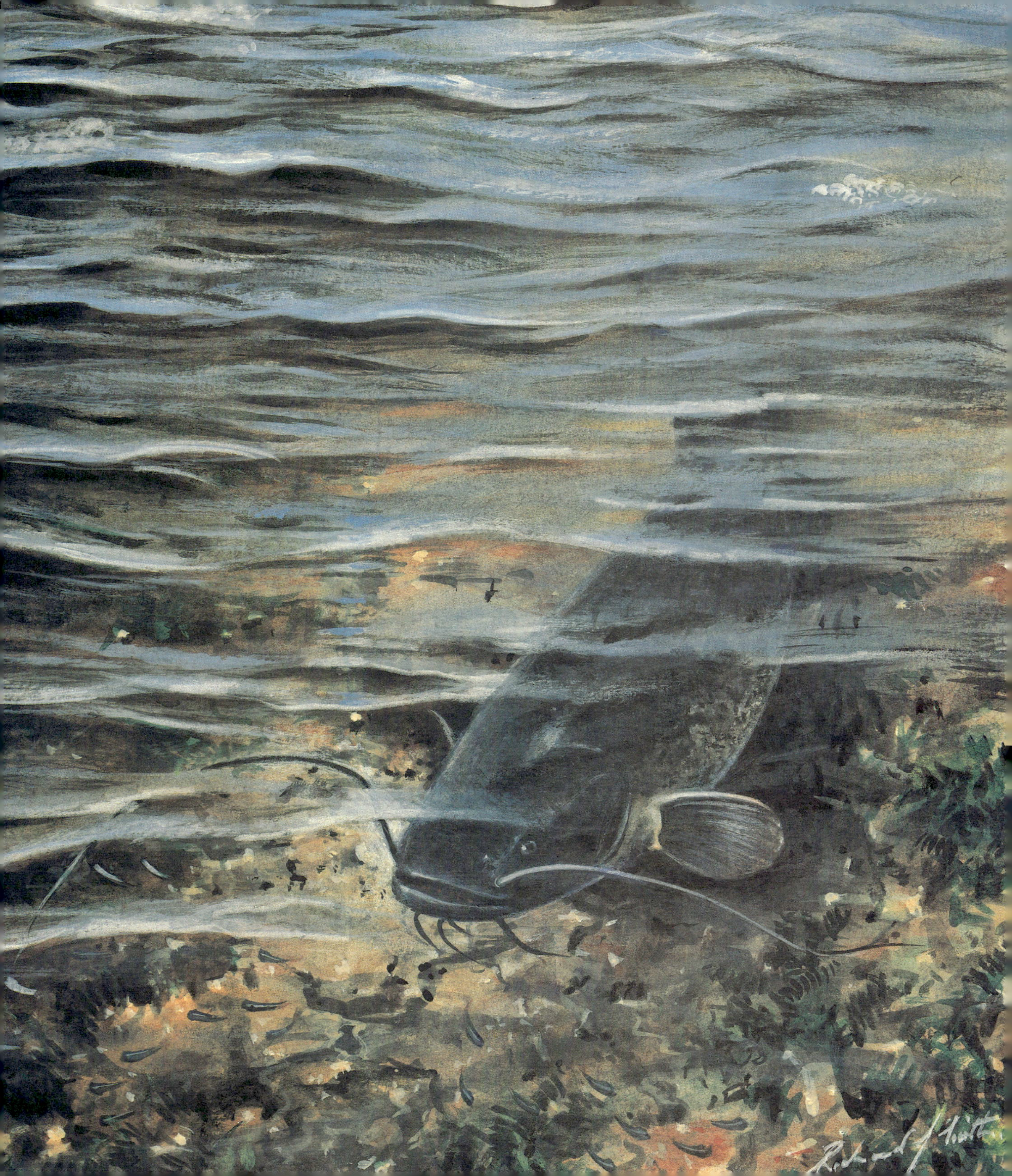

GOLDEN SUMMER WITH THE NEGLECTED GIANT

The summer of 1983 was, I suppose, my first really serious attempt to catch a big *Silurus glanis.* I had fished Claydon Park in 1981 on about six occasions and although I caught on all but one of those days a 'double' somehow eluded me.

It was not until July '83 that I returned to Claydon. I had rung John Golder the previous day and he kindly offered to obtain a club ticket for me and so my plan was to fish for three consecutive days. John greeted me in the car park with my ticket in one hand and a big smile beaming across his face — he was amazed at the fact that in my keenness I belted past the car park at 70mph! John was not alone and he was quick to introduce me to two other catfish maniacs; Bob Baldock and Glyn Owen. I didn't realise at the time that all three would become such good friends. I hardly noticed the long trek across the field for I was trying to get some information out of John about the feeding habits of the Claydon 'cats', before we went our different ways. With John and Glyn set up opposite Bob, who'd pitched in at the dam end, and myself, about 20 yards to Bob's left, we had the small lake well covered.

I had thought hard and long about rigs and baits for catfish for it was common knowledge that on hard fished waters, such as Claydon, the catfish fed suspiciously and were quick to reject a bait if they felt any resistance. Indeed, John Golder had already mentioned this in his catfish chapter in *Top Ten* and had given full details of several rigs which he'd found effective. It was obvious that many anglers fishing for catfish blanked because they put very little thought into their set-ups and this was proved by certain anglers like John, Glyn and Bob, who caught on a fairly consistent basis. They would use set-ups which gave very little resistance to a taking fish and this meant freelining where possible or where small, weightless baits were used the casting weight would be attached with PVA. Also, drop off indicators were employed in conjunction with Optonics, or no bite alarm at all. This type of set-up certainly helped but from my many years' experience with shy carp I reckoned that the 'cats' still mouthed their baits often without getting caught. My logical thinking process had been put into motion time and time again about this situation and I decided on the following baits and methods: I wanted a bait which hadn't been used for 'cats' before that had a good, strong smell and one that didn't appeal to other species, such as carp, which are more than plentiful at Claydon. My first choice was raw squid — I used this bait in 1981 so I knew it would work. I was also aware that it hadn't been used before, and I hoped not again since! A body section of squid, about 1½ inches long, was attached to the size 2 hook via a 2½" length of half pound nylon. The 30" braided hook length was attached to a 2½ ounce fixed lead. This meant that the catfish could pick up the bait in its lips and feel absolutely nothing. It could then take it into its huge mouth with confidence and, as the fish moved away, the heavy fixed lead would cause it to panic, or feel the hook point, either of which would result in a proper run. It was great fun sitting behind the rods knowing that such a set-up had almost certainly never been used for catfish.

I didn't have to wait long before one of my indicators whacked up against the rod and line poured from the spool. For the next five minutes I played a catfish but made no impression on it at all until, unfortunately, the hook pulled out. I had definitely lost a personal best, and was very disappointed. I'd given the fish quite a lot of stick and this resulted in it fighting harder than normal so I decided to play the next one a little lighter. An hour later Bob showed me how it's done and he landed a really lovely wels weighing 16-14 which had taken a small livebait. The following six hours remained uneventful and John and Glyn packed up at 4pm. They could hardly have driven away by the time the 'cats' began to feed and within a short time I caught a six pounder followed by an $18\frac{3}{4}$. Bob was keen to measure the larger fish as it looked very long and after recording an amazing length of $4\frac{1}{2}$ feet we returned the fish aware of the fact that it had almost certainly been an upper '20' at sometime in its life. That evening, on departing, I groundbaited the area with about 25 pieces of squid ready for my return in the morning.

My keenness to return the following day caused quite some havoc for the local police. Apparently, I'd driven through one town so fast that a local police car gave chase but couldn't catch me! This was explained to me when my Dolomite Sprint was forced to stop at a road block some eight miles further on. It was very difficult trying to tell eight police officers at 3am that the catfish were almost certainly feeding and that it was imperative I be there at first light! That day, and the following, proved to be very worthwhile and I finished up with eight catfish; 18-12, 18-4, 12-4, 11-8, 10-12, 10-4, plus two singles. Bob fished the three days and caught four 'cats' and John Golder returned on the last day and had two nice doubles, so all in all it was a very enjoyable session. The catfish caught by Bob and John had all taken small livebaits fished on braided hooklinks whilst my catches were half on squid and half on livebaits.

    I was so impressed with these whiskery 'monsters' that I decided to devote the remainder of the summer fishing for them and I was back again the following week for another three days. Not unlike the previous week, the weather was ideal for 'cat' fishing — clear skies, very hot with a light breeze and in the following three days I hooked nine 'cats', the two best weighed 19 and 17 pounds.

    Bob and John didn't do as well as the week before but one fish certainly highlighted the session and made me determined to fish on. Barry, a friend of Bob's, joined us on the second day and at 11.30am, fishing the shallows, he hooked his first double figure 'cat' and what a fish it turned out to be. After an incredible ¾ hour fight, he landed a fantastic 28 pounder. Barry was amazed at the 'cats' performance — at one stage the catfish ran up to the extreme shallows and, whilst trying to bury its head in the mud, about three feet of its body waved in the air! I was astounded — it was the first big wels I'd seen and I challenge anyone to see such an impressive fish on the bank and not dearly wish to catch one himself.

The following week I could visit Claydon for only one day and I arranged to fish with John Golder. For me it was non-stop action all day and I landed eight catfish the best weighing 17 pounds. John, fishing two swims to my left, had a lot less action but managed one double and a really handsome fish just over the 20 pound mark.

Besides seeing Barry's '28' and John's '20', I had heard of at least two other big 'cats' which had been caught during the weekends, so this together with my good 'run' made me determined to fish on — I now wanted to catch a '20' badly.

Towards the end of July the catfish became reluctant to feed at all and this was no doubt due to the 'hammering' they'd received over the previous weeks. Indeed, the fish had fed so well on livebaits that at one stage anyone could catch them. I fished on my own for two days at the end of July and although I caught some nice doubles, it was definitely getting harder, everyone was blanking and only the sheep were feeding.

At this stage of the season John decided to stop fishing for 'cats' because he wanted to concentrate on other species and after some discussion, Bob and I decided to team up. This seemed the most sensible thing to do as we both thought alike and by now the fishing at Claydon had got so difficult that 90% of the anglers had given up and we knew the going would be harder. We decided to fish Claydon three days a week for the following month as a final concerted effort to get amongst the bigger fish for although Bob had caught a '20' elsewhere that season, a big Claydon fish had eluded him also.

Four days fishing during the first two weeks in August produced no fish whatsoever. This was the first really difficult period and not a single catfish was caught by anyone for several days.

The 'cats' wouldn't look at livebaits or deadbaits. The squid had stopped working too but this was probably due to the fact that I had made no secret of the bait and many anglers had been 'flogging it'. It was our third visit in August and Bob decided to use a new bait. This is where I lacked experience for I wasn't sure if the problem was bait or whether the fish were feeding at night when we were not allowed to be on the water. Bob's many years of experience with catfish convinced him it was bait and he proved this by catching fish of 16-18 and 9-12 on sausage portion. Bob doesn't miss much either and he was quick to point out that both fish had guts which were completely packed full of food. This sparked off many hours of thought and discussion. The 'cats' were obviously eating something, but what? We eventually decided that it probably wasn't livebaits, unless they were feeding on them exclusively at night, and that it must be a natural food. We took mud samples from the lake bed and quite amazingly not one living organism could be seen although we appreciated the fact that some sort of food might be plentiful in certain areas only. The one source of food which was plentiful around the lake margins was mussels and after looking at the 'crusher' in the back of the 'cat's' mouth one could appreciate how easily the whole mussels could be crushed open. Of course, mussels, which have always been regarded as one of the best 'cat' baits, had been used on and off by anglers that season but I don't think anyone was trying them at this stage — in fact there were by now very few anglers fishing the water. We decided that a change in tactics was needed for the last day and Bob quickly collected about 60 mussels. Most of these were de-shelled and thrown out into an area about 15 yards by five yards as darkness fell. We slept in our cars that night and started fishing at dawn the next day. Our four rods were baited with mussels and cast into the ground-baited area where considerable bubbling was evident. It wasn't long before something picked up the two whole mussels with which I'd baited the right hand rod, causing the indicator to lift slowly up the needle and the line to gently uncurl from the spool. The fight that followed was most impressive and half an hour later, after a tremendous display of tail waving whilst the fish tried to bury its head in the mud, Bob relieved my aching arm by netting our first 'biggy'. The fish measured 52 inches in length, had a girth of 23 inches and tipped the scales at a satisfying 26¾ pounds. It was my 26th catfish from Claydon that season and after seeing and hearing of so many people catching big fish I was obviously relieved. Going by the very rough inner edge of the main pectoral spines the fish appeared to be a male and its lower jaw was deformed so that when its mouth was closed it protruded much further than normal — it was about 1½" more proud than the upper jaw.

Before I had time to brew a celebration cuppa Bob was locked into one of the most amazing fights I've ever seen between angler and fish. I should explain here that Bob suffers from rheumatoid arthritis of the hands and he cannot afford to play a fish for too long as his knuckles gradually seize up. After six or seven minutes Bob had made no impression on the 'cat' and I could see from the expressions on his face that he was already in pain. I don't remember how long it took to land the fish but just watching Bob wore me out! We were of course convinced it was another '20' but we should have known better — it was a fish we knew as 'Trees' and it weighed $15\frac{1}{4}$ pounds. The reason for its name is that the fish's right hand main feeler splits into several 'branches' and looks rather like a bare tree. Both John and myself had caught the fish earlier in the season and not unlike on this occasion it had put up a tremendous fight.

During the following weekend. Bob and I discussed our plans for the next week. Every snippet of information was pieced together and our observations and thoughts helped us formulate a plan. That session I caught three 'cats' up to 16 pounds and lost one but Bob caught his 'dream' and if anyone deserved it, it was he. On the second morning, following another baiting session, Bob caught a nicely proportioned fish of $22\frac{1}{2}$ pounds but before he could sit back to appreciate his hard slog for a '20' from Claydon that season he was hell bent into another big *Silurus glanis*. Another keen fight followed and as I lifted the fish out and onto the bank I recognised it, as the big one I'd caught the previous week, by its deformed jaw. It had picked up the same bait in the same spot. We weighed him in at 26-10 a personal best for Bob — and then set about the difficult job of photographing a pair of 'twenties'. For many years Bob had hoped to catch a brace of 'twenties' and now his dream had come true.

I had studied the many bubblers at Claydon over the previous three visits and it appeared that there were two sorts. One type were mainly largish bubbles with odd smaller ones and these were confined to a small area of approximately nine inches in diameter with occasional clouding of the bottom silt — these, I believe, were caused by the many carp which, incidentally, never seem to stop feeding at Claydon! The other type of bubbles were larger patches, between 12"-24" in diameter, of small bubbles and these were often in the deeper water and nearly always associated with heavy clouding of the mud. This latter type I believed to be caused by the catfish and I proved this by catching two 'cats' very soon after casting to such bubbles. Another interesting observation made at this stage of the season was that the 'cats' were beginning to avoid the lines in the water and tended to feed beyond our furthest casts and to both sides of our lines no matter where we fished. This problem did not exist earlier in the season because the lake was being heavily fished all over and the 'cats' had to put up with anglers lines wherever they went. We partly overcame this problem by casting to bubblers and moving about more often. By the time we later worked out a solution there was no need to put it into practice for the water temperature fell slowly over the following weeks and the 'cats' started to feed more confidently.

Although we had caught well on mussels during our baiting schemes the carp had also got the taste for them and were becoming quite a nuisance. A new bait was called for; we had previously tried scallops, black pudding and crayfish to no avail and so we decided to try some big boiled baits which Bob left me to make up for our next trip. 300 boilies about $1\frac{1}{2}$" diameter were made from liquidising Birds Eye beefburgers with eggs and then stiffening them with semolina, wheatgerm and Casilan. A two minute boil hardened them nicely.

A very cold misty atmosphere was prevalent when we started our next session at Claydon and the water temperature was now 60°F. A local angler informed us that he had been there every day since our last visit and that no 'cats' had been caught. We baited with about 30 boilies and I put both rods on the new bait whilst Bob fished one with mussel. 15 hours later as darkness fell Bob reeled in his baits after a biteless day for both of us. I decided to give it a few more minutes which turned out to be a wise move for I soon had a nice steady run on the right hand rod; the burger boilie produced its first 'cat' and it weighed 14 pounds. This gave us a little more confidence and we threw in another 60 baits hoping that the 'cats' would find them during the night.

The following day we both used the boilies but again only one run was forthcoming; it was Bob's turn this time with a $12\frac{1}{2}$ pounder at 5.30pm. Unfortunately, the small carp were by now picking up the large boilies and so we decided that in view of this and the comparative lack of action from 'cats', that we would use mussels again on our last day. Unlike the first two days of the session the final day, which was the 1st September, started off cloudy and warm with a light variable wind. Bob decided to fish the tree stumps swim at the dam end and I fished the wide swim near the bushes halfway along the house bank. Three hours passed and I strolled along to see Bob who kindly offered me a cup of tea. As I sipped the 'liquid gold' my eyes nearly popped out of my head for I could see a mass of bubbling all over the area where Bob had his baits and the grin on his face told me that he was fully aware of the fact. I went back to my gear and considered moving towards Bob's end of the lake as there were no 'cats' bubbling in my area. I thought about it for a few minutes and decided to move as we'd seen this type of bubbling before and big 'cats' were responsible. I was just about to reel in one of my rods when I happened to notice Bob standing amongst the rushes with his rod well bent into a fish. I walked along and as I stood alongside we guessed it was a good fish for it was hugging the bottom and sending up big clouds of mud. Twenty minutes later I slipped Bob's big landing net under the fish and the battle was over. We laid the wels on the soft grass behind the swim and it was a magnificent looking fish, well proportioned and in immaculate condition. It tipped the scales at 22-2 and to say we were pleased would be an understatement. Later, at 4.40pm, I placed a bait on a bubbler I'd seen about 25 yards to the left of my pitch and caught a $15\frac{1}{2}$ pounder and just as the light failed Bob scored again with a 10-pounder — a pleasing end to our three day session.

The second week in September saw us back at the lake again and little did we know what was in store for us. We'd agreed that another new bait was needed and I suggested to Bob that we try cockles for we had not heard of anyone using them before. Unfortunately I didn't attempt to get the bait until the day before our session which happened to be a Monday. After three hours of driving around I gave up and settled for frozen sea mussels from a supermarket. Bob was just as determined as I to give the new bait a try and on hearing the bad news when we met at Claydon he decided to drive into Buckingham that morning to the market. An hour or so later Bob returned with about 2½ pounds of cockles — he'd found two stalls and bought all they had! That day I fished with one rod on sea mussel and one on a cockle and our only runs came as the light faded. All three bites were on my rod baited with sea mussel and the result was a 10 pound 'cat', a 10 pound carp and a lost fish. I didn't like the idea of carp picking up the bait so soon so I decided to stop using the sea mussels and that evening we baited with cockles.

Day two saw another cold start with a clear sky and no wind but by mid-morning it became milder with a light south westerly breeze. At 10.30am I caught a very small 'cat' and as the morning wore on conditions looked perfect — the water temperature was rising nicely (the water temperature often varies up to 10°F between day and night at Claydon) and a little further out than I'd cast, considerable bubbling was evident. I reeled in both rods and carefully placed my baits amongst the feeding fish by overcasting and gently reeling back. This was advisable for the bubbling nearly always stopped when a bait splashed directly on top of them — not surprising in just two feet of water! I brewed a nice cup of tea and sat back in my chair very confident of a take from one of the bubblers and my thoughts drifted back over the past few weeks of the summer's 'cat' fishing and the immense enjoyment I had got from it.

The peaceful relaxation was soon broken by the screech of my buzzer and I leapt forward and struck into the culprit. As the rod buckled over there was a huge swirl from what was obviously a very big fish. For the first ten minutes or so the leviathan worked its way up and down the far bank. This caused me some embarrassment for the two anglers opposite kept reeling their rods in and re-casting once the 'cat' had passed through their swim only to reel in again a minute or so later when it returned. After they'd done this about ten times they eventually came round to our side of the lake to join in on the fun. I suppose it was after about 20 minutes that I suspected something was wrong about the way the fish was fighting. It had felt quite normal at first but the fish was not showing any signs of weakening and to be honest it was doing exactly what it wanted. I will not dwell on the subject too long but after $1\frac{1}{2}$ hours every muscle in my body hurt and I could fight the fish no longer. There was no alternative but to hand the rod to Bob whilst I could have a rest. I was frightened to look at the rod at times as Bob really laid into the fish but after seven or eight minutes he'd also made no impression on the 'thing'. Eventually, two hours five minutes after hooking I pulled the 4'7" catfish into the net. We removed the hook, which was lightly embedded in the underside of the fish and I checked the mouth for any hook marks but the only one that was evident didn't look that fresh. The fish weighed $31\frac{1}{4}$ pounds and had a girth of 22".

We had no further action that day which was just as well after such an incredible battle. We talked about it for a long time and wondered what it would be like if the same was to happen in the middle of the night when you might be on your own! We packed up at 8.30pm and before making our way back to the car I baited the area with some cockles. By 5.30am the next morning I was fishing the same area again. Both rods were set up with running link leger arrangements and I'd baited one with two cockles and the other with a mussel foot. Although there was evidence of 'cats' feeding near my baits I wasn't sure whether I wanted to hook one or not! After the experience the previous day, plus a rough night in the car, I decided to play it hard from start to finish but this approach didn't help very much for it seems the more stick you give a catfish the harder it fights! The fish worked its way up and down in front of me and after about 15 minutes of giving and taking line it showed the first signs of weakening and came close to the bank. It then moved off to my left with the clutch clicking slowly and I could foresee a slight problem. The 'cat' was heading towards the bushes which overhung the margins in this one spot. Normally they are no problem as one can easily hold the rod up and walk past the bushes making sure the line passes over the top but for once this was not possible as the fish was only inches from the bank. I tried to turn the fish as it got under the bushes but all effort failed. These catfish are absolutely amazing fighters — I shudder to think what tackle would be needed if it was imperative to stop a big fish — the fight of a big carp is simply not in the same class. The 'cat' got right under the bush and eventually everything went solid. Bob and I were surprised that this happened for we knew there was very little in the way of twigs and branches under the bush. After a bit of fiddling I managed to get the rod and line over the bush and then tightened up to the fish from a new angle. This manouvre succeeded and I heaved the 'cat' onto the surface complete with a small branch which had caused the problem. Bob slipped his big net into the water and as the fish neared him I got a glimpse of it and commented that it looked a reasonable fish but nothing massive. As always with Bob, he made the netting operation look so easy, when in fact it's not, and as he lifted the fish out we were both surprised at its size. Bob carried it back to my pitch and I quickly sorted out the scales and weighing sling whilst he removed the small hook. Bob slipped the catfish into the wet sling and lifted up the scales. '30¼ pounds' he said, and I burst out laughing. I told him to stop mucking about for it was obviously a low to mid-twenty — or so I thought! Sure enough Bob had read the scales correctly and after deducting the weight of the sling it weighed an amazing 29¼ pounds. I couldn't believe it after the trauma of the previous day and it was quite some time before I accepted the weight.

That was our last very big catfish of the season. We fished at Claydon on several more occasions and continued to catch well until late September when I decided to return to carp fishing. The last fish we caught there were at a water temperature of 56°F and it seemed obvious that they could be caught at a much lower temperature. Glyn Owen visited Claydon in late October to witness a '20' plus fish and others, and Bob and I saw signs of feeding 'cats' in mid-November when we fished on a mild day.

Around this time, when the water temperature was 52°F, Bob caught several small 'cats' from another water. There have been many reports of anglers accidentally catching catfish at Claydon throughout the winter when conditions were mild and I think it is now only a matter of time before someone goes to the trouble of 'cat' fishing in the winter months and proves the old beliefs wrong. The problem is that Claydon can not be night fished and winter days are short — the best choice would probably be Tiddenfoot. One thing is for certain, no matter how experienced an angler you are, until you have spent a summer with the 'Neglected Giant' you have missed out on something very special.

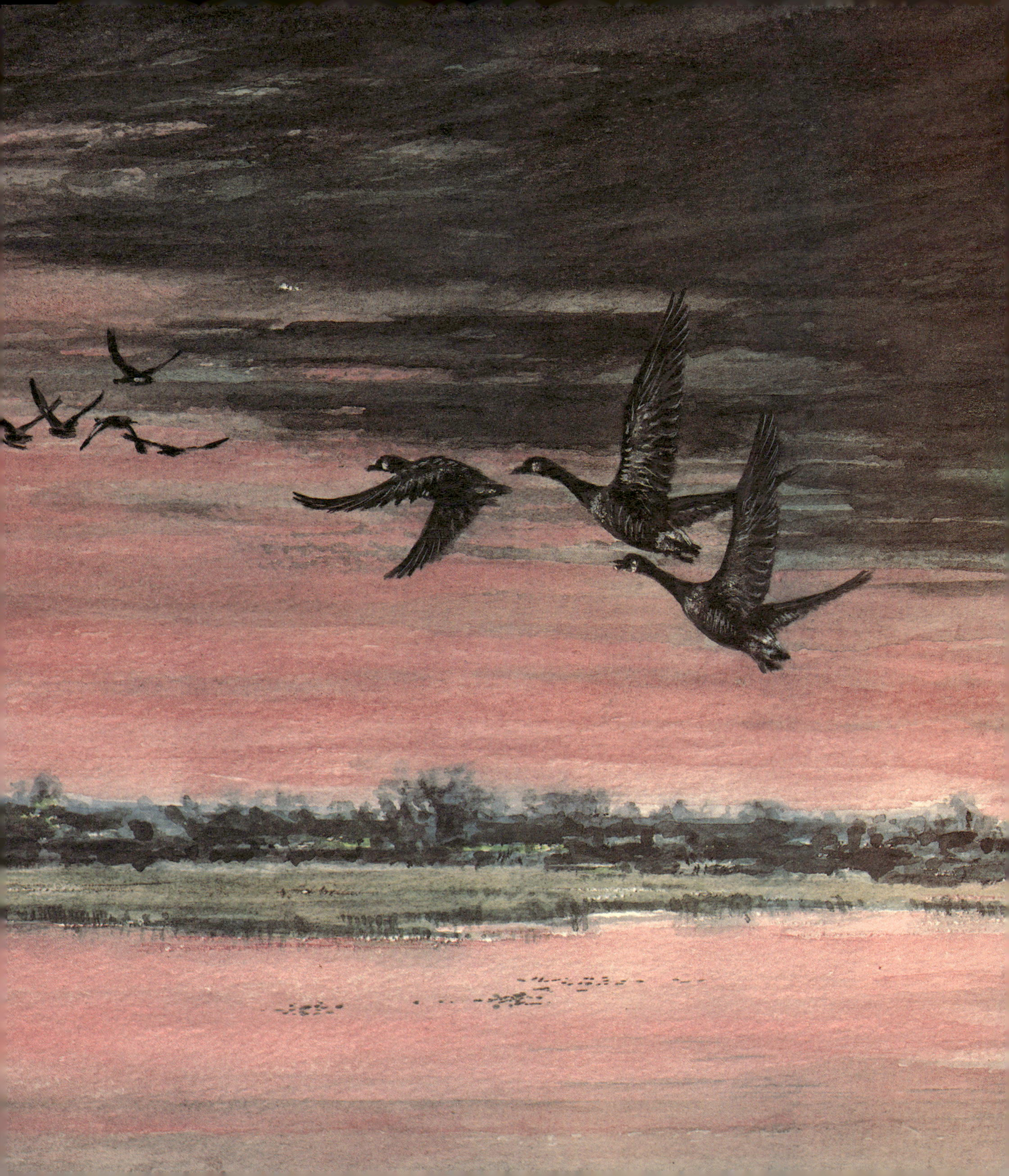

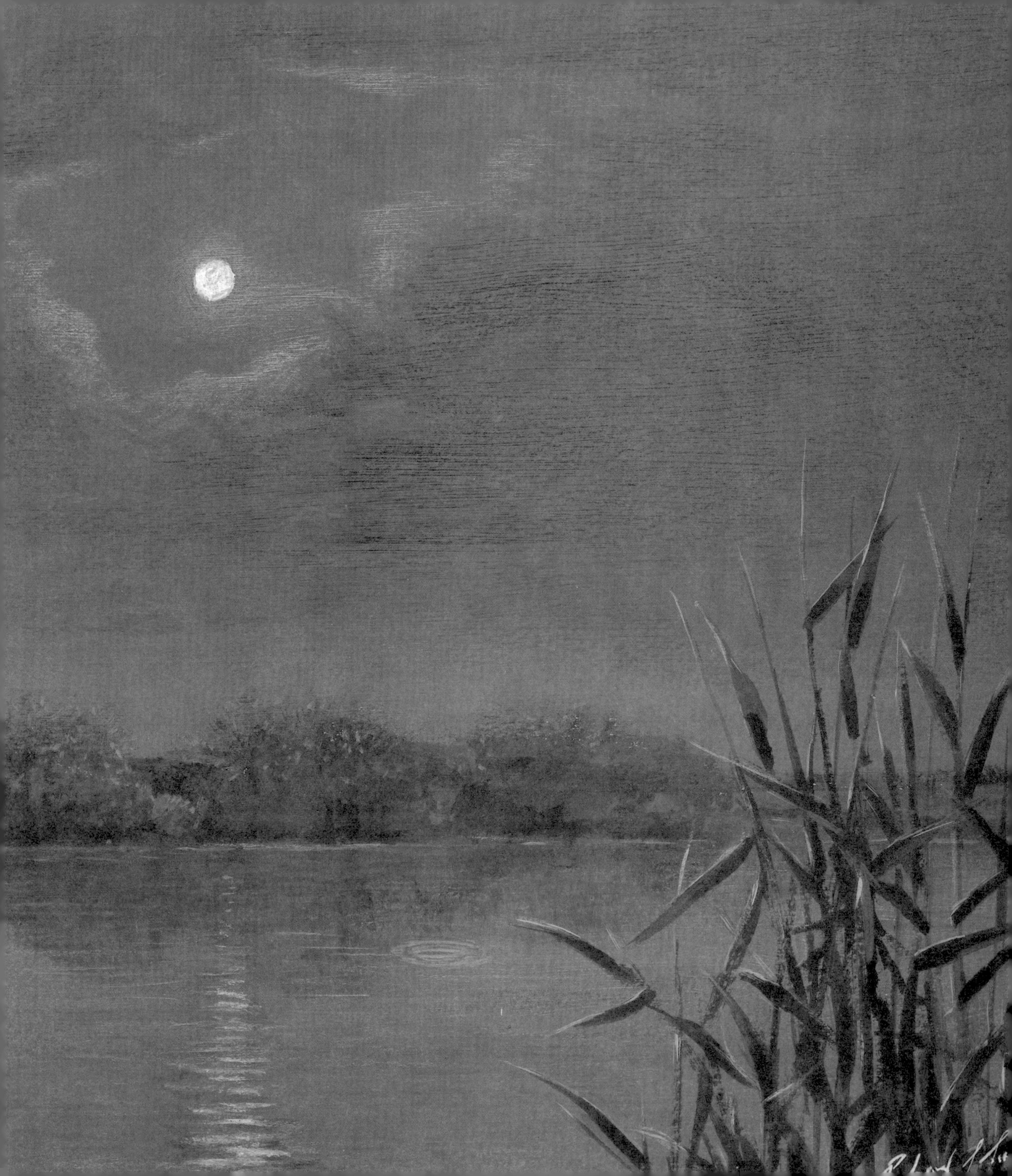

Duncan's

I first met Duncan Kay at Waterways in the 1970's. I could soon see that he was a good carp angler, because he often got three or four doubles, when, at that time, I couldn't catch any. Although I realised he was a bit of an odd character, I respected anyone who could catch good carp. At this time Duncan was stocking his own water with some of the Waterways fish. I should like to say here and now that many people thought that he was obtaining these carp illegally, but this was not so; the fish were for sale at the time, and Duncan has the cheque stubs to this day to prove that he bought the fish. Needless to say, this was kept a bit quiet because there was a syndicate on the water, and the person selling the fish didn't want the members to know they were being sold, for obvious reasons.

    I didn't get to know Duncan well at this time, and many of the fish he put in his own lakes, the Mid-Northants carp fishery, died when he stocked the lake with imported fish which contracted the carp disease called erythrodermatitis. I know that Duncan was restocking with other fish, including some more from Waterways; the next thing I remember is seeing a report in one of the angling papers that someone had caught a '30' from Duncan's — this was obviously one of only four survivors. This fish was caught in June 1976 and the report made me want to fish the water. I telephoned Duncan in September and asked him if there was any chance of fishing as a guest. He agreed and I had a day at the lake, where I caught a 14 pounder. I kept phoning Duncan and getting trips and I caught 33 doubles in the next four sessions, including my first ever 30 pounder.

There are two lakes at Duncan's fishery, which he has always called 'The Pits'. One is about $4\frac{1}{2}$ acres in size and the little one alongside this is about an acre. Pits they certainly were in those days; they had been dug in the thirties to provide material to build the A6 road bridge over the River Nene, and they were very barren, with no trees or bushes round them. Today they are very different, with plenty of cover.

The main lake is a sort of 'L' shape, with a wide end containing most of the shallow water, ranging from 3-6' with the rest of the lake being 6-8 feet deep and flat bottomed. There are fields surrounding the lakes but the main road is not far away, and the lights from the road and from some factories are quite strong at night. This was the year of the great drought when many waters dried up completely and the lake was about three feet below normal level. There was some marginal weed, mostly Canadian pondweed, although it was not too thick in that year.

I was very successful at Duncan's from the start, and was soon catching many more fish than the other members who fished there. This was because most of them fished close in, often with float tackle, in order to avoid the weed. I soon noticed that many fish were jumping in the middle of the lake, so I made up my mind that this was where I should put my baits. When one of the local members saw that I was going to cast out into the middle with a 2oz bomb he was amazed: "That will frighten all the fish. You must be mad", he told me. I soon found that there were small areas, often not more than two feet across, of clean gravel bottom amongst the slightly silted bottom, and it was on those that the carp fed. Fishing in these clear areas I had an enormous number of fish, and I still catch in this way on the water today; people have often wondered why, and this is the reason. The clear gravel areas occur not only in the weed, but in places where there is no weed at all. Most of the bottom is covered with a thin layer of silt over the gravel, but it is the clear gravel areas which the carp like. I know exactly where these feeding spots are, but other anglers had not seemed to have found them. Sometimes they had good catches by dropping accidentally on these harder areas, but as they hadn't identified them, their next session was often blank, as they did not fish in the clear areas. Their catches were very inconsistent for this reason, whilst I got fish regularly.

Another reason for my success at the time was the baits I was using, and the method of mounting them. Many anglers were using boilies as I was, but they put them on with a baiting needle and pulled the hook right into the bait. They laughed at my side-hooked boilies, which I mounted with a large hook sticking out of the side, but this method hooked far more fish and I had the last laugh.

When there was no-one there I often put in 1,000 small Yestamin boilies, and I'm sure they all went quite quickly — I usually soon caught fish in spite of there being so many baits out. For some reason I always felt quite guilty at putting in so many baits, I nearly always had a run before I got all the rods set up; I even had a system for setting my landing net up with one hand. I was catching around 100lbs of carp on each trip, and while I was a guest also — no wonder I became unpopular! I found this by far the easiest 20's water I have ever fished, and even to this day I have found it the same — except for Redmire of course, which was even easier.

I went about 6 or 7 times as a guest and Duncan was very pleased about my catches, as he had wanted to prove to the members that the fish were there to be caught, even though they hadn't been catching many of them. Duncan then held a meeting where he said that he was thinking of offering membership to me in the next season. Most of the members present were against this. When Duncan asked them their reasons for wanting to keep me out, they came out with all sorts of stories about my fishing which were quite obviously untrue, and it didn't take Duncan long to realise that the real reason they wanted to keep me out was because I had been so much more successful than anyone else — so he promptly rang me up and offered me membership, which I accepted.

In spite of the fact that some members hadn't wanted me to join, no-one was unpleasant in any way once I had been accepted, and in fact this soon became my favourite water. The fishing and all the members were very pleasant, and Duncan managed to run a good syndicate where all the members, some of whom were not carp anglers, got on very well together. It must be remembered here that Duncan had not taken over an established carp fishery. There were no carp in the water at first, so he built up the fishery from scratch. I enjoyed my fishing there for many years, and have always been grateful to Duncan for this. He has always been able to mix a certain amount of light-heartedness with a fishery which provides an average for carp of over 20lbs; there can be very few waters in the country where the average weight is so high. Over the next two years I fished the water regularly and caught many fish there. One session I remember was the one in which I had an exceptional catch. It was the 18th June 1979, and I had been at Ashlea Pool in Gloucestershire. It was hot and many fish were on the top. Until now I had foolishly believed what all the members had told me, and this was that the carp at Duncan's wouldn't take floaters — so I hadn't tried them. On this occasion, I had a lot of boxes of Felix Meaty Crunch (now no longer made) in my car and I was determined to give them a try. I set up my gear in my usual pitch on the beach, with the intention of not bottom fishing until it got dark. I went up to the other end of the lake and catapulted in some floaters, which, to my surprise the carp started to take immediately. I didn't begin till 4pm and had two lower doubles by 8pm both on the floaters. After catching the second fish I went back to the swim and put out the bottom baits

Within a few minutes of casting out a new bait, which was ground up pilchard flavoured Munchies, mixed with a little Casilan and eggs, one of my most successful baits, I had a good run and hooked a big fish. This carp kited very fast and hard to my left, where it buried itself in a marginal weed bed. Although the weed is soft I needed some patience before the fish eventually came out, and I held the rod high and waited for it to move. When it did so, I pulled it towards me, where it fought doggedly for about ten minutes. It was duly netted and weighed at 30lbs 5ozs. I had another double at 1am, with nothing else during the night. Next morning was hot, sunny and calm. I started stalking at 1pm with FMC, having put out a lot, and I had three fish from three different areas of the lake; they weighed 18lb, 15.12 and 15lb. The first and third fish were both commons. This was great fun, and if I had sat in my swim I should almost certainly have had nothing.

    I went back to my pitch at about 8pm once it had cooled down, and settled again for the night. I had another double almost immediately, and at dawn, about 5am, I had another good take on my left hand boilie. This fish got me out of bed, but it was worth it; it proved to be a leather of 33lb 5oz, at that time a new record for the water — and my second '30' in two days. I had another double during the morning on the floater, but by this time most of the other anglers on the lake had gone up to the shops to buy the Felix Meaty Crunch and were trying it all over the lake. I packed up and went home after a very good three day/two night session.

The ten carp I had weighed nearly 200lb, so I ended with a very good opening spell for the season, which had started very badly for me at Ashlea.

Many anglers ask me to describe the syndicate waters I've fished and whenever I'm asked about Duncan's I think of the high winds that one often encounters there. It is certainly subject to much stronger than average winds due to its position in the valley close to the River Nene. The valley tends to funnel the winds into a narrow area, making them much stronger than usual, and I have had many brollies smashed to pieces there. Despite this, I always fish the windiest spot and even to this day Duncan is always amazed when he finds me facing the teeth of a very strong cold wind. Often I have been unable to set-up a brolly and have sat out in the driving rain all day and all night. I can recall many stories of fishing in these conditions such as the day when a hooked fish 'kited' along the lake and the huge bow in the line, caused by the gale force wind, forced the fish to beach itself some 20 yards up the bank! Geoff Kemp will no doubt remember his only trip to the water; he started by hanging huge steel bar hooks on his rods to keep them on the rests but finished the day with his rods laid on the ground held down by whatever he could find to lie on top of them, including his feet. I was fishing at the time on the causeway which separates the two lakes and is only about three yards wide — I had a run, leapt up to strike and to my horror the wind lifted my bedchair, complete with sleeping bags and pillow, high into the air whereupon it came crashing into the middle of the little lake. All I could do whilst playing the fish was watch the whole lot sink slowly to the bottom. Geoff found this totally amazing but I had the last laugh when he decided to have a pee — talk about get your own back, he was soaked!

I have had many enjoyable and interesting carp fishing sessions at Duncan's lake, but it would be boring for the reader if I related many more of them here. There is one trip that I must include, however, as the happenings on that trip were quite unique; since I have already written about this session in my book *Carp Fever*, I think it is best if I just repeat the story here.

It was August 1980 and I had arranged to meet Peter Mohan at the Mid-Northants fishery for a 24 hour session after an invitation from Duncan. I arrived at 4am and eventually settled into a swim we call the 'small beach', situated alongside 'Alligator Point' in the SW corner of the bay. It was overcast and very hot, with a light southerly breeze and as the morning passed it became obvious that I could not expect to catch using bottom baits in these conditions; some stalking was called for. Walking round the bay I catapulted about a quarter of a box of Felix Meaty Crunch onto the surface where I had seen some carp cruising and basking. Whilst setting up a stalking rod back at the swim I could see fish responding well to the free offerings. Huge backs broke surface as the baits were being taken — the conditions were perfect. It didn't take me long to get into position in the bay with the light wind behind me. The carp were feeding in and around the weedbeds at a range of about twenty yards. I quickly 'superglued' a single F.M.C. to the back of the hook shank and cast to the fish. With this presentation the hook hangs under the water and the carp usually prick themselves as soon as they touch the bait; a small piece of weighted peacock quill served as indication and casting weight. Although they were taking free floaters confidently I only had two takes in the next hour. Both fish were landed, and both were doubles.

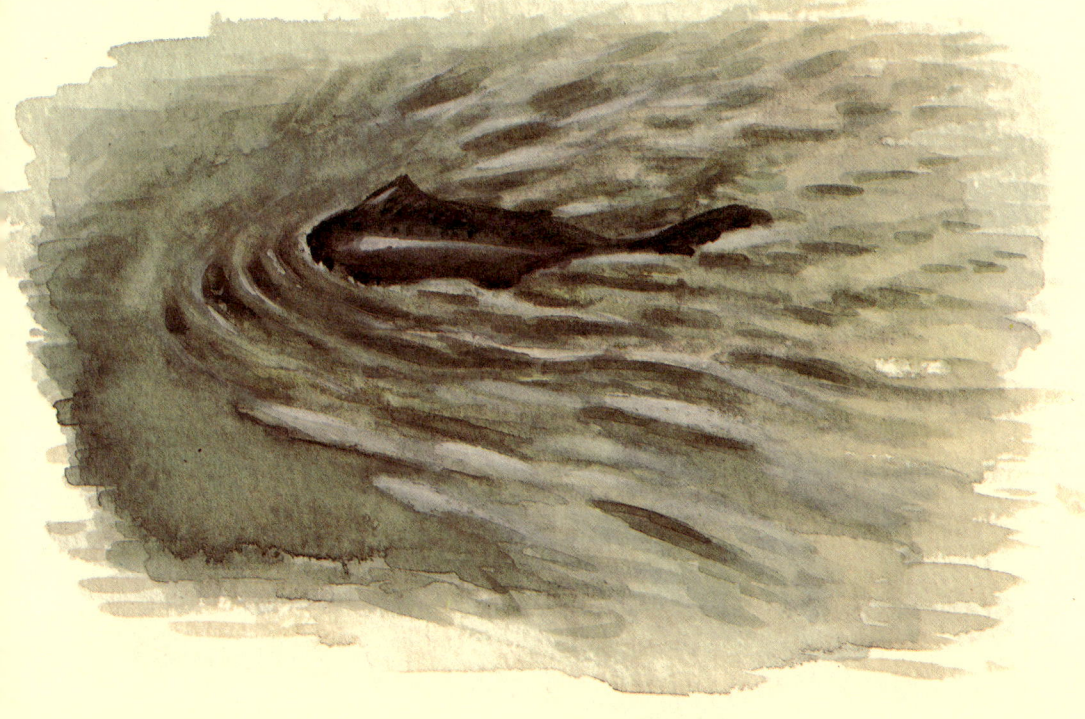

As the evening approached I wound in and sat back to watch the fish for a while. I soon noticed one very large fish swimming amongst the others; it was a leather which looked to be about 30 pounds. I was quite surprised at this for I had never seen a fish of these proportions taking floaters on this water before. I sat for a while, working out a way to catch the fish. I could not get my tackle to drift the 40 or so yards to where the fish were now feeding due to the surface weed. My thoughts were interrupted by the arrival of Peter's car at the top of the field. We quickly got talking about the fish and I showed him where they were feeding. However, by the time he had sorted his gear out, the clouds had thickened, the temperature dropped and the fish had moved off.

Peter settled into a pitch opposite me and just before dark it started to rain heavily. Anticipating a wet night, I carefully positioned my baits in a clear gravel area 40 yards out as my intention was to leave them in the same spots until daylight, for accurate recasting during darkness would be difficult. After scattering some thirty hookbaits in the area I settled under my brolly and brewed a cup of tea.

A little later the clouds darkened to an ominous grey and it began to rain heavily. The distant thunder became louder and the heavy rain which had started around 8pm became an intensive downpour, the like of which I had never seen before. Rain lashed the surface of the lake and vivid streaks of lightning were followed by massive claps of thunder. I could clearly see Peter on the other side of the lake holding onto his umbrella for dear life.

It was 12.30am when my buzzer first sounded. Although confident of some action I had forgotten about my rods as I had been employed full time in attempting to keep dry. At first I was a little surprised. For a start I didn't want to come out from under my brolly and secondly, I just couldn't understand why a fish should feed with the ground shaking from continuous violent thunder and non-stop lightning flashes. Anyway, the first part of the fight was no problem as the fish gradually worked its way in and out of the weed beds coming towards me. I sunk the other rod tip so as not to pick up the line, but the rain was so intense I could hardly open my eyes, and was completely soaked to the skin within two minutes. The water was running down my neck, past the more vital areas (urgh) and ending up in my boots and it eventually actually began to come out over the top of them. The fish moved to the left so I squelched my way to the side of the swim. About a minute later I heard a faint voice to my right. It was Peter on the other side of my brolly. He was almost shouting and it was only after three increasingly louder replies that brought him to my side. The noise of the rain pounding the water was absolutely incredible and the loud conversation went something like this:-

'Oh, here you are. I wondered where you'd gone. I couldn't see you from behind your brolly. Hell of a storm isn't it?' said Peter.

'Yeah, it's fantastic'.

'I can't stand it any more round there, the wind's blowing it right into my face and I'm drowned. I've packed my gear, I thought I might as well as nothing's happening.'

'Yeah', I said again, trying to pay attention to the feel of the rod.

'Had any action?'

'Not a lot, just the one take'.

'Oh, you had a take did you — no good?'

'Yeah, it feels reasonable, moving quite slowly'.

'What. Have you got a fish on?'

'You should know', I said, 'you're standing right next to me'.

'Crikey, I couldn't see — the rain's so heavy. I suppose I might as well wait to see it. How long have you had it on?'

'About five minutes'.

The fish moved further to my left and started to take line from the clutch much to Peter's amazement, for he doesn't allow such things. A minute or so later he said:

'Don't you play your fish for a long time. Do you know, the longest I've ever played a carp for is 12 minutes?'

'Yeah, but how many thirties have you played', I said jokingly, not having the slightest idea of how big the fish was. I couldn't even tell how much pressure I was putting on it. Another couple of minutes passed and Peter, who by now was also like a drowned rat, assured me of an execution if it wasn't a thirty. After a very dogged fight in the margins I netted the fish and hauled it onto the bank. Sure enough it was a very big leather. We weighed it by torchlight together and agreed on a figure of 30 pounds 14 ounces, although I said I would weigh the fish again in the morning because of the rough conditions. Peter swore at the weather and departed.

I recast and by about 3am the rain stopped. I was wet and

very tired and now all was quiet I decided to jump in my sleeping bag until light. The wind dropped and I quickly went off to sleep dreaming of all the things carp anglers do — naked women and huge carp. However I was just getting into my first dream when a terrific clap of thunder made me leap up. This time the wind had changed completely and the storm was returning. After repositioning my gear I somehow managed to drop off again and the next thing I knew about was a wet feeling all along my underside in the morning. I opened my eyes and could hardly believe it; the lake had risen THREE FEET during the night! Originally my gear was well away from the water's edge, but I was now completely surrounded by water which was up to the underside of my bedchair despite its extended legs. The first thing I looked for was my boots which I leave standing up next to my bedchair. I couldn't see either of them so I felt around under the water and located one. It was pinned against the underside of my bedchair. I just didn't know what to do as I sat on my bed chair with a wet posterior. I knew I was going to have to step into a foot of water. I then looked across the lake and burst out laughing — there was my other boot, floating out in the middle of the lake. It was all quite extraordinary and as I looked at the swim around me I could see my food box, gas stove, one piece suit, tackle bag and everything else was either completely under water or floating around. Carp were even swimming around in the adjoining fields.

After retrieving my gear from the lake, I weighed the fish again and just as I had expected the fish had lost a quarter of a pound after four hours in the sack. I settled for a weight of 30.10, took two photographs and returned the fish before organising a rescue operation which lasted all day. I shall never forget that 'thunderstorm thirty'.

Apart from the unusual sessions caused by the weird weather that seems to surround the fishery at times it became a very important 'testing ground' for me. I often used it as an experimental water and as explained in *Carp Fever* it was from there that I landed the first ever carp to be caught on the 'hair rig'. Besides this perhaps 'historic' capture I spent most of my hours experimenting with new baits, rigs and tackle whilst keeping incredibly accurate records. I spent a whole season using two mixes of a boilie; one contained a blend of amino acids, which I had spent more than 3,000 hours 'perfecting' in tank tests and the other was exactly the same bait but with no aminos. The two baits were fished equally in every way for the same amount of hours and swapped to a different rod every time a fish was hooked. Results were recorded for a whole season thereby removing chance captures but at the end of it all both baits caught exactly the same amount of fish! Then there was the amino bottles. An amino acid solution was poured into a small jar with a screw-on lid. Stones were included to make sure they sank and the caps were perforated with holes to allow a leak-off. During initial trials I introduced a bottle into the baited area every few hours but after much effort this had no measurable effect. Subsequent trials included the introduction of Alka Seltzer tablets to force a faster dissipation of the aminos but again to no effect. Several of the other combinations and single aminos which proved effective in my tank tests were also tried but to no avail and so ended my many thousands of hours and hundreds of pounds expense on yet another 'dead end'. In retrospect, it's a good job it didn't work otherwise bottle bars would now be more common than gravel bars! I could probably fill a small book with the tests I carried out at Duncan's including the very effective 'Twitcher Hitter' which I dropped after deciding it was unethical but I don't wish to bore you.

Some people may wonder why I don't fish Duncan's as much now, although I still remain a member. I find that if I fish a small water and start catching the same fish over and over again, as I eventually did at Duncan's — so much so that I was able to recognise and even predict the actual weight of the fish before putting them on the bank — that I get bored, and this is what happened at Duncan's. I thought it best to give the water a rest for a while until the situation had changed, so I don't go there very often now, just one or two trips in February each year. But I shall be back; unless I have to, I don't contemplate ever leaving the syndicate whilst I am still carp fishing, and I am very grateful to Duncan for allowing me to be a member of a water where I have so much enjoyed my carp fishing.

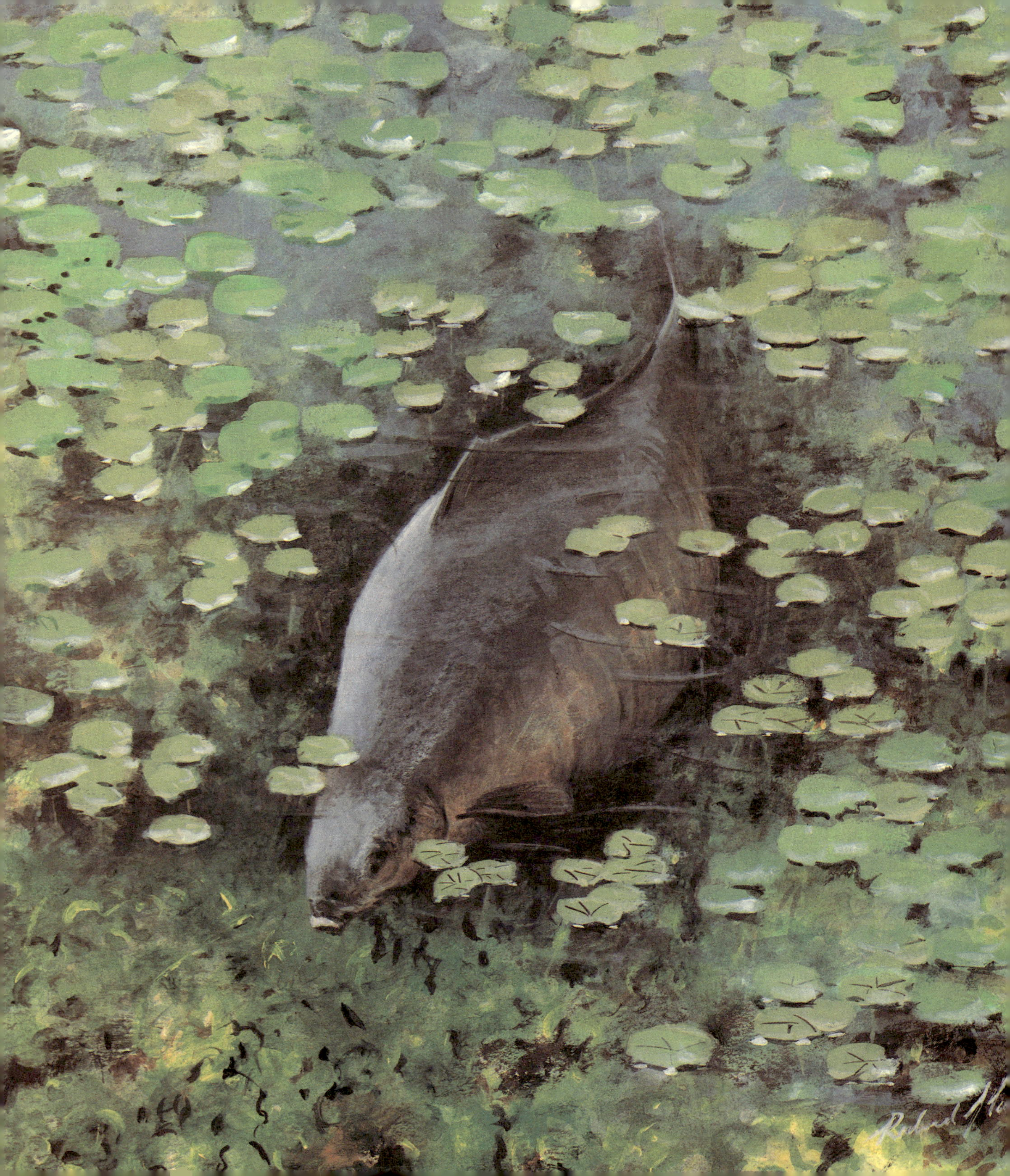

Ashlea 2

My third year in Ashlea, 1979-80, was rather different from the others. I was so determined to catch 'Lucky', the other big thirty, that I went on every one of my rota weeks from the start of the season, a total of ten sessions, which took me up to the end of October.

I certainly had an extraordinary start to the 1979 season. I went to Ashlea on June 16th and both the known thirties were caught on this day. I was lucky enough to be opposite Vic Gillings with my new movie camera when he hooked one of them, which weighed in at 37¼lbs and was a new record for Ashlea Pool. I filmed the whole thing, and this is now on record on the famous film, *Ashlea Record*, which many carp anglers have seen. Geoff Booth had the other fish at 33½lbs later that day, and with two thirties caught I decided that it would be better for me to go home the next day. When I got back, I phoned Duncan Kay and asked him if his thirties had been out yet; he said that they hadn't, so I went straight up to his water — and caught both his thirties in the same session, along with eight other doubles. I had seen four thirties on the bank, two of which I had caught myself, in as many days, and on two different waters!

On my second visit to Ashlea I started with an uneventful day fishing floaters, but the following morning I hooked and lost a very good fish. I had spent the night fishing in No.18, which was to become my favourite swim at Ashlea, and from which I caught most of my good fish, including Humpy. This swim was nearest to the house and today no fishing is allowed from it. It is at the deeper end of the pool and the ground had been cut away in preparation for the building of another hide which, fortunately, was never finished. This meant that you were able to fish low down with the bank behind you. Although the water is fairly deep here the weed is very heavy and no holes in this weed were visible from ground level. From a tree, however, two tiny gaps could be seen, and it was not easy to position the baits in these gaps, which is, perhaps, the reason no-one else fished there.

    I hooked a fish at 5am one morning which picked up a bait I had carefully placed in a tiny hole in the centre of the pool alongside an overhanging ash tree. On hooking the fish, the rod was almost wrenched out of my hand. The clutch never gave so the fish had no choice but to come towards me. As it did so, it buried its head deep into the cabbages and a great line of bubbles came up until all went solid after some five yards or so. After about a minute of heaving, my line cut through the cabbages until I was at a direct pull to the fish again. Slowly the movement of the fish became more apparent until I managed to heave it clear. Once in contact again I got the fish on the surface, but still some 10 yards away from my confined pitch. The swirl on top was a sight for sore eyes, sending waves across the pool that lapped the opposite bank where my friend Len was putting in the Z's on his well-worn camp bed. Surely that'll wake him I thought, but those who know Len will know the answer. Determined to land the fish I really laid into it, with the strong tackle, but exactly the same thing happened again and all went solid. This time it took me a couple of minutes, but I managed and the struggle was set back in motion. Boy, did I give that fish some stick — more than I'd done before with any fish. Despite this, the fish's action was uncanny; it was behaving with incredible determination. I don't know where the fish got the strength from, but it almost pulled me in as a long line of bubbles once again rose to the surface and the fish became solid yet again, for the third time.

    I just couldn't believe it, normally with a pokey rod and extreme pressure one can keep the Ashlea fish on the top and clear of the weeds — but not this one, he was different. I suppose it must have been another, very frustrating, minute before I carefully got the line to cut through the cabbages, hoping and praying the hook would hold. The still motionless fish was now about twenty feet away from me but more to my left and I knew that if I got it free again it wouldn't have far to go before it would reach an underwater mass of sycamore branches to my left. As I bent the rod double I began to feel the movement of the fish again and a wave of confidence flowed through me. Sure enough the fish came free and the fight was on yet again. I could now see the fish in the clear water and the adrenalin really pumped round my body. After three years fishing Ashlea I believed that I could confidently recognise all of the fish and this one I'd never seen before. Everything was again put to the test; as the carp thrust its head from side to side, the pressure on the tackle began to increase. The $2\frac{1}{4}$lb carbon rod was reaching its limit and I was again stunned at the strength this fish had and just as I was expecting something to break, the clutch, very slowly for the first time, paid out some line. Apparently the adjustment I'd made, hooked onto the fence the previous morning when setting-up, was perfect, and the dependability of my Cardinal 55 proved itself. The fish gradually got nearer to the sycamore branches and the next move was imperative. As the fish was almost there I gave the clutch screw a quick half-turn and it was now up to the fish to break me or give in. I fully expected a break. The fish gradually lifted up through the water until its head and back broke the surface and it rolled completely over, its underside reflecting the early morning sun. As it rolled, its body just clipped the branches and the tree gently tremored. What a beautiful fish it looked and as it moved across in front of me only a few feet out, I got a good, long look at it. Its flanks were brilliant orange and it was very long, I would guess three feet or slightly more but unfortunately it had no depth to match its length. Its head was rather bull-nosed in shape leading up to a jet black shoulder and back. As the fish got to my right it turned towards me under the now subdued pressure and was obviously beaten. A few turns of the reel and the fish was now close and ready for the net. Then, for no apparent reason, the hook just fell out.

    Words cannot describe how I felt, I was really sick. I watched the fish, which was motionless at first, gradually turn and slowly swim off, itself not knowing exactly what had happened. Lifting my head a little higher I could see Len was still asleep, unaware of the whole situation, yet so close. It seemed that the fish and I were in a complete world of our own, fighting each other with incredible determination on both sides, fighting like wild animals and no-one else knew about it. I toyed with the idea of telling nobody as I felt so ashamed, but I knew Len would sense something when he'd come round and ask if I've had any action. Even today, some six years later, I am still disappointed about losing that fish!

A few hours later I hooked another fish in the same spot which behaved in the normal Ashlea manner under heavy pressure, and was soon on the bank. This fish meant absolutely nothing to me and I could have quite easily returned it without weighing or photographing it. I knew the fish I'd lost would have been an unknown one, one that had never been landed before and to me that would have been a terrific achievement, regardless of its size. I spent the rest of the day stalking, as most of the fish appeared to be on the top, but I couldn't get anything to take a floater. I had left my tackle at 18, and by 8pm I was back there again, to find two fish bubbling in the swim. I got the baits out and had another fish on the right hand rod within 15 minutes; it weighed 19½lb, although this meant little to me as I was still suffering from losing the big fish earlier. This was the only time that I have been really upset by the loss of a fish, and this was especially because I am almost sure the lost fish was an unknown that has never been caught before or since, although it may have been seen.

During the next four sessions I caught four fish, two of which were on floater and two on bottom baits, but the largest was a common of 17¾lb; the bigger fish seemed to be avoiding me at this time.

It was mid-September when things seemed to change. I adopted my normal stalking tactics with floaters, putting in boxes and boxes of FMC, a method which had been so successful up to now. At about mid-day I had a 20.12 mirror and as usual I returned to bottom fishing for the night. I cast a bait actually into the cabbages, and at 3.45am had a 20½ pounder. This second fish, which we called 'Little Fatty', was one of the most difficult fish in the lake to catch, only coming out once every two or three years. It had a deformed backbone, was blind in both eyes and had no dorsal fin. It was a very active fish, either continually boiling in the deeper water, or tail waving for up to seven days and nights at a time in the shallows! The ducks used to peck at its dry tail as it stuck out of the water in the shallows. Without success most of the syndicate members had tried to catch this extraordinary fish whilst it was preoccupied with natural food. I remember once spending a whole day trying to catch it after several other members had given up and becoming so frustrated when I failed that I threw a house brick at it, which at least made it give up tail waving for a while, though I didn't hit it. I was obviously very pleased when I finally did succeed in catching this fish and it was then that I discovered why it continually 'boiled' and tail waved. The fish was a floater! Whilst releasing it I found to my amazement that I could not easily push the fish under the water and when eventually it managed to swim downwards, as soon as it eased up it floated to the surface. At first I thought the fish might have temporarily got some air trapped in its bladder, but this was not so. 'Little Fatty' remained in this condition for two years; continual feeding was necessary to replace lost energy and eventually, one day in 1982, she could keep it up no longer and died.

Until the start of the colder weather I continued to catch fish, with three more up to 20.10 but the bigger fish still eluded me, although I doubt if anyone at Ashlea had ever caught so many carp in a season.

At the start of the 1980 season I decided to change my
tactics completely, and to fish under the cabbages, however
thick. After three years at the Pool I knew just about everything
about it, and was determined to get that really big fish; it could
only be a matter of time before I hooked it.

After two days of not seeing any fish as so often happens at
Ashlea I decided to climb the tree on the dam, and from here I
caught sight of a fish in the rushes at the shallow end. I climbed
down again, got a rod and my landing net, and very slowly
walked out into the water and through the rushes. It wasn't long
before the fish, which was Lucky, caught sight of me and moved
slowly away. I followed it, the cool water coming just over the
top of my waders, and eventually came to a two foot diameter
hole in the rushes which we had not known was there. In the
clear water were four fish — Lucky and Humpy, both 30's, the
common and an upper double; there must have been over
80lbs of carp in this tiny space, all swimming round and round
in a circle.

Now I was in a dilemma; how could I select one of the
biggest? I soon realised that this was not going to be possible, so
very slowly — remember I was in water to the top of my
waders, and only six feet from the fish — I pinched a piece of
breadflake on the freelined hook, and dropped it gently into the
hole. As it sank, I saw a mouth engulf it, so I struck. The fish
was hooked, but there was an enormous amount of splashing as
it and the others shot out of the hole in all directions. The
hooked fish went deeper and deeper into the reeds, which
slowed it up and I was soon able to net it; it was the smallest of
the four, of course, at 16lbs 10oz. This did however serve the
purpose of forcing the big fish out into the lake from where it
had been hiding!

The following day I had a fish on floater — and it was the
same fish again — obviously it liked me! By the time I returned
to bottom fishing I found that fish were bubbling underneath the
cabbages, and I had already given a lot of thought to the
problem of how to get at them. The bait would have to be
presented on the bottom under the cabbages so I fixed a two
ounce Arlesey bomb to the line with a link swivel which was
stopped by a small Berkley swivel tied in the line. A baited
hook, on a six inch tail was then tied to the bomb using PVA
strips. The hook point was left bare as usual and was masked by
a PVA pad formed by folding the PVA. This bolt rig would sink
through the thick leaves, coming to rest on the bottom. I
attached a matchstick to the line by means of a float ring about

a foot less than the depth of the water; as long as this was not on the surface I knew that I had got the bait through the cabbage leaves and onto the bottom.

I introduced free offerings by painstakingly tying each bait to a stone using PVA — a long and laborious task — and that night I had a double using this method, which proved that it was working. The method also worked for me during the next couple of sessions, when doubles were caught each time. After nearly four years I was catching well, but I still had not caught the big fish I had worked for, although I was confident that it was now only a matter of time.

My next rota was my fifth session of the season, and was the culmination of all my hard work at Ashlea, for it was during this session that at last I caught the fish I had waited for so long. I have described the capture before in *Carp Fever*, and since I can't make it happen differently readers would no doubt like me to repeat that description here.

On the 15th September I arrived at Ashlea Pool for a three day session, a session I was never to forget. The one and a quarter acre pool was looking its best, the water was gin clear and the lilies were just beginning to weaken, for in a month's time they would all be dead. A breeze was blowing towards the deeper end of the pool, making it impossible to spot the fish properly, so I climbed a tall sycamore tree overlooking the spot where I thought the fish might be and soon spotted several large carp, two of them clearly over thirty pounds; one of them was the big fish I wanted. They seemed to be swimming in a clear patch amongst a mass of dense weeds, and every so often they would sink out of sight below the mid-water lily leaves and bubble profusely. I put some floating baits in the swim up wind of them but as the baits drifted over their heads they showed interest. So, by about noon, I set up two rods in the swim nearest to where I had seen the fish. My plan was to fish one into the clear hole and the other right in the thickest part of the dense patch of cabbages.

The bait was a special concoction which I had used with remarkable success on several waters since the previous winter. It consisted of: three ounces of Casilan, three ounces of Complan, one ounce of Lactalbumin, two ounces of C&G baby milk, one ounce of wheatgerm and one ounce of castor sugar. this was added three eggs plus 15ml of cream/butter flavouring. Each bait was rolled into quarter of an inch balls and dropped into boiling water for one minute and then left to harden for a full 24 hours.

I cast a bait into the small clear area without problems but the other bait needed to be presented on the bottom under the cabbage leaves if I was to stand any real chance of success, for this is where the carp were obviously feeding. I had put a lot of thought into this problem and set up with rigs as mentioned previously. This bolt rig had the effect of blasting its way through the thick leaves coming to rest on the clear bottom under the cabbages. Although I was initially worried about the line rising vertically through the cabbages I decided that once a fish did pick up the bait the bolt rig would make it run and disregard any possible line resistance caused by the upward path of the line.

Once my rods were set up I baited the area heavily and sat back and waited. Around 2pm that afternoon I had a line bite which I struck at and spooked the fish concerned. The rest of the carp immediately followed and from then right round until the following afternoon nothing happened.

That afternoon I carried on stalking and was given the first opportunity in four years to have a definite chance of catching the fish I was after. I had spotted the big leather while up a tree and decided to have a go for it. I climbed down the tree but lost sight of the fish because of the 'chop' and glare on the surface of the pool. However, I was determined to catch the fish, so leaving my stalking net at the bottom of the tree I took my rod and some bait back up the tree with me. I immediately saw the big leather again and quickly dropped a small free offering of bread-flake in front of the fish. As the flake sank slowly the fish moved forward and took it. I couldn't believe my eyes. I gently lowered a second piece of flake, this time with my hook in it, some 15 feet down to the fish. As it sank the fish followed it down, looked at it for a while, circled it, touched it with its lips and then decided it wouldn't have it.

I don't really know what would have happened if I had actually hooked the fish. On reflection I intended to throw my rod into the water, after hooking the fish, and immediately jump out of the tree into the same spot. I then proposed to get hold of the rod, hoping the fish was still on and continue to play it standing in four feet of water — a dubious proposition!

By evening all the fish had returned to my original swim and were feeding like mad on the baits I carefully introduced. I had tied each free offering to a stone using PVA to give it a better chance of reaching the bottom. I settled down for the second night confident that something was going to happen. I baited the swim and set up a third rod to cast out to another spot where bubbles were continually rising.

After dark it rained heavily and I immediately lost confidence but when it finally stopped around midnight, the wind dropped and it got very cold. The signs started to look right and I knew I was going to get some action. Around 2am had a six-inch lift on my left hand rod, but nothing else happened. An hour later I had a couple of four inch twitches my 'extra' rod. This didn't develop into anything immediately but 30 minutes later I had a jerky lift on the bobbin. I struck straight away and met with solid resistance. It was pitch dark and I had no idea what was happening, I couldn't feel any movement or see the rod tip and so I thought I was weeded. I kept the pressure on, feeling fairly confident that the fish wou move, and a few seconds later the bobbin on my left hand rod started to rise. It then dawned on me that the fish had slowly kited across in front of me, maintaining an uncannily even pressure. The swim was very confined and I knew that the fis was near the sunken branches of the sycamore to my left so I lowered the rod tip into the water and 'pumped' the fish back Within 30 seconds it was on top and ready to net. The gap in front of the swim was only three feet so it was necessary to n the fish over the top of the other lines. I lowered the other roc off their rests and picked up my landing net, but as I pushed t net forward over the top of my rods the mesh became entangled. Not being able to see what I was doing as it was so dark, I struggled to disentangle the mesh from the rods whilst keeping the fish on top using the other hand. This went on for about half a minute and I decided that I would never do it unless I could pull the mesh and rods back away from the wa into my pitch which would be impossible with one hand, so I then released the bail arm, dropped the rod onto the ground a nipped round the back of the swim to get my stalking net. Under the circumstances it turned out to be the best thing to and luckily, when I got back the fish was still on. Because the net was only 30 inches wide I had to kneel down, peer into th darkness and wait until the fish's nose touched the spreader block of the net. When I was sure the fish was over the net I lifted the surprisingly heavy fish out and put it on the ground the back of the swim. I kept looking at the fish trying to decid how big it was and I just simply had no idea as it was so dark got my small pocket torch from my kit bag and switched it on only to have it fail immediately. The battery must have got we from the rain. For a few seconds I didn't know what to do as was keen to know what fish it was before sacking it. I couldn'

en weigh it without the torch. I thought it must be a thirty. ter picking it up again with my heart pounding I very gingerly t round the lower bone of the tail to see if it was only half gth, as the 33 pound mirror I caught two seasons previously d an old tell-tale scar. As my fingers felt round the lower bone a ve of excitement flowed through me — it wasn't the mirror so could well be the big leather I'd been hoping for for so long.

I decided to carry the fish in the weighing sling back down e lane to where my car was parked with the intention of ighing it using the headlights. As I walked down the lane I pt saying to myself 'I've got you at last, you bugger', and ondering if it might go 40 pounds.

I lowered the fish onto the ground in front of the car, itched the headlights on and pulled the weighing sling back. It s the big leather. The scales registered just under 39 pounds d after deducting the weight of the sling the true weight was ¼ pounds, my biggest carp ever. I then sacked the fish until st light when it was witnessed and photographed before being urned to its weedy home.

The four years of hard work had been fully rewarded. The afternoon was a sad one for me as I knew when I glanced back at the pool on departing that I might never fish the water again. My plan was to move onto new waters, although I might well regret this, and at the end of the season I left the Ashlea syndicate.

I really enjoyed my four years at Ashlea, and I should like take this opportunity to thank Peter Mohan for allowing me to spend so much of my time during those Ashlea years fishing in such pleasant surroundings and in such a pleasant atmosphere. Ashlea is a unique water; there is nowhere like it, and it will always remain for me the place where I have had some of my most satisfying and frustrating carp fishing ever, and this was not only because of the size of the fish, but because the syndicate was always well run, with none of the jealousy and unpleasantness which seems to take place on many other waters. I tried harder at Ashlea than at any other water I have fished, with many sleepless nights, and with so much hard stalking that on three occasions I literally fished myself into a state of collapse in the hot sun. I worked hard for all my Ashlea fish . . . but it was all worth while when I weighed in my personal best. Had there been big fish there which I had still caught I would still be a member today; as it is, I can only hope that the current members appreciate their Ashlea fishing as much as I did.

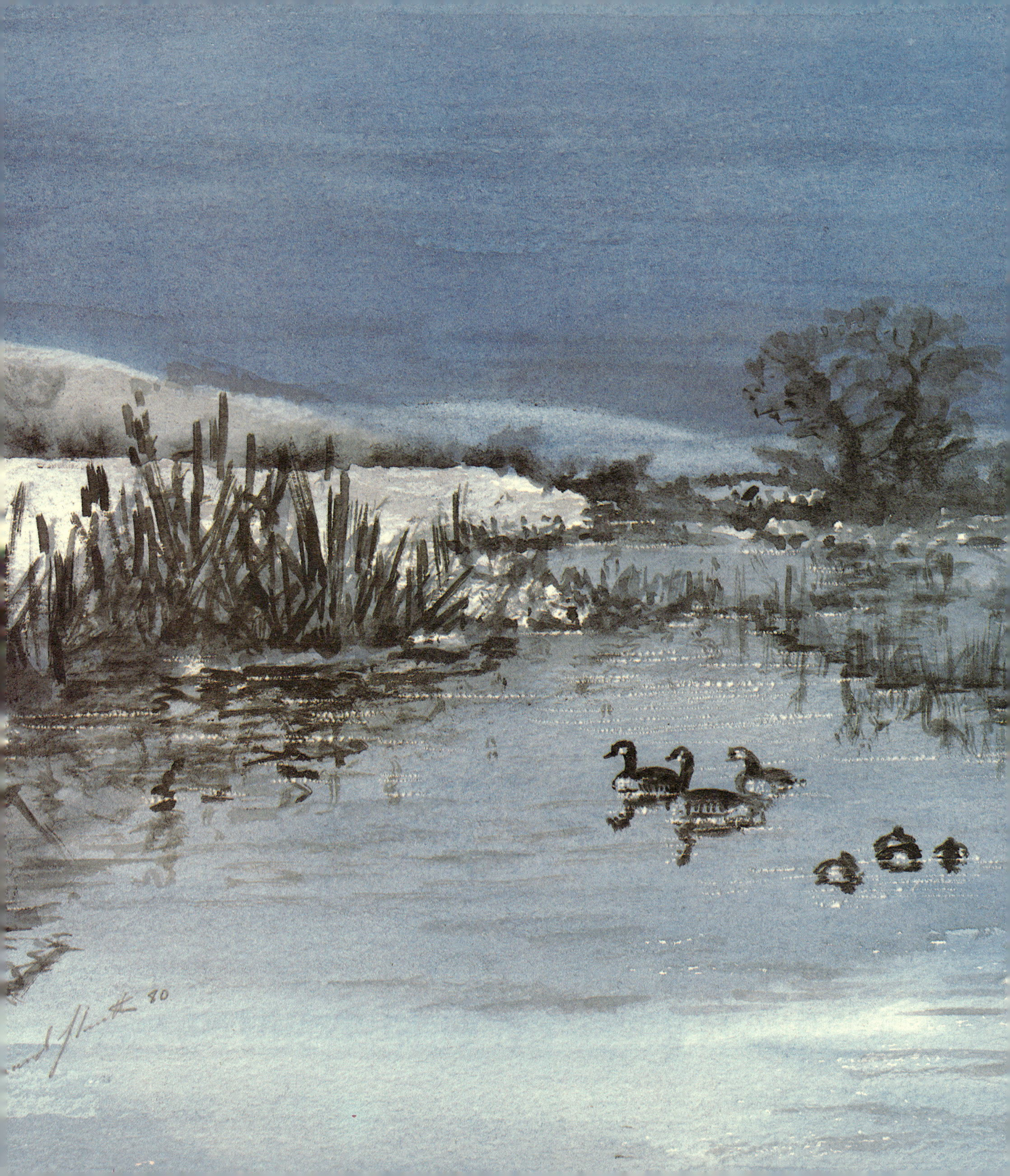

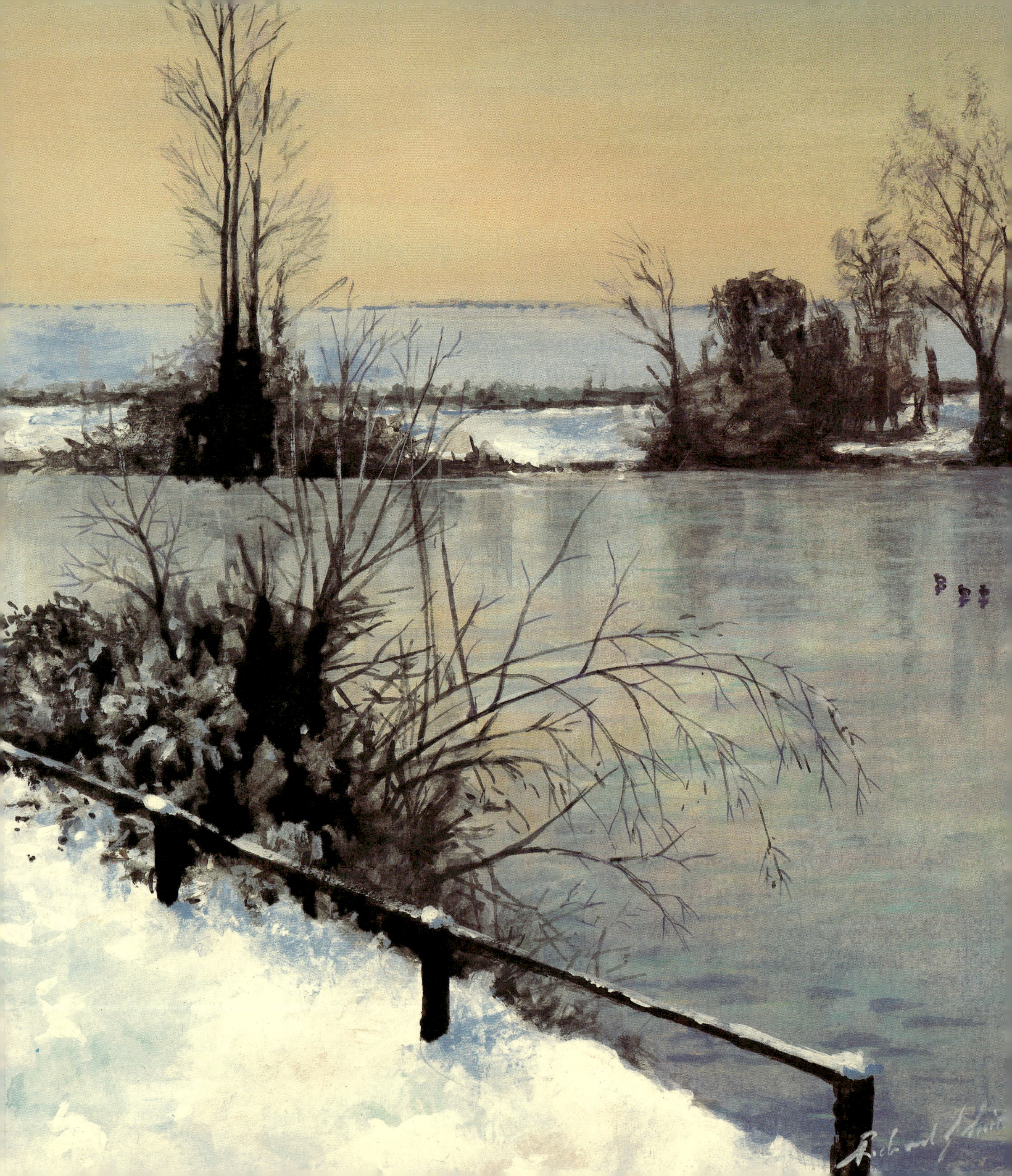

REDMIRE WINTER

Throughout Redmire's history only a handful of carp had been caught in the winter. It seemed that more often than not the reason behind this was because no one could be bothered to fish there in the winter months — a fact which I find quite amazing — one of the best carp waters in England totally neglected for half a season! However, some anglers had fished occasionally in the winter and their results were a little encouraging for the time put in. My plan then was to visit the pool every third week, keeping to the normal rota arrangements and to fish for a period of three days and two nights.

Early November found me at the pool and although it was officially winter as far as carp fishing is concerned, the weather had been kind. Odd shrivelled leaves still remained on some trees, the water had only slightly coloured and the green holly bushes made it feel like autumn. I arrived at 7.30am and within ten minutes of standing in the Stumps swim I saw two fish roll three quarters of the way across between the Stile and Kefford's. A few minutes later I was standing in the Willow Pitch — a swim I was keen to fish as it had produced so many carp throughout the summer and although I'd caught carp from virtually every swim I had yet to fish a session in the Willow. Therefore, the sight of a rolling carp easily convinced me to fish there, but as I was making my second journey across the dam with the final load I saw another fish move out from the Stumps. I was in a dilemma. A choice had to be made and quickly. I dropped the remaining gear in the Willow swim and stood there for a few minutes watching the water for further signs. Nothing else showed so I walked round the lake to the Stumps again and amazingly carp were 'head and shouldering' every 30 seconds or so. Watching these big fish was enough to send shivers down your spine — uncannily each one stuck half its body out of the water but slid back in again without the slightest sound. Only the merest ripple could be seen on the calm water. It was as if they really wanted to let all hell loose but for fear of man they had to control themselves.

By 10am I had at last set up, my choice being the Stumps. I positioned two baits three quarters of the way across the pool towards the Stile and Keffords; those were cream flavoured boilies about $\frac{1}{2}$" diameter. I mention the size because when I first joined Redmire I was led to believe that the carp would only take very small baits but as the season wore on good catches increased my confidence and I soon found that the Redmire carp accepted these larger baits. The third rod was baited with a single tiger nut and carefully positioned amongst a hundred or so free offerings twelve feet out. All three baits were in about four feet of water — I didn't want them in deeper or shallower water because I found the depth of water fished at Redmire to be very important. I had noted that on virtually every feeding spree all the fish fed at the same depth wherever they were, be it at the dam end or the shallows and this would be at a particular depth somewhere between two feet and six feet depending on various factors, the main one being temperature. In fact I never caught a fish in more than six feet of water despite placing baits in the deeper, centre channel on many earlier occasions. The fish I had seen priming were definitely feeding on the bottom and here it was about four feet deep. After my lines had settled I pulled off an extra four feet of slack from the rod tips so that the lines laid nicely on the bottom. I was using fixed leads so a tight line wasn't needed but more importantly it was pretty obvious from tree top observations throughout the summer that the Redmire carp avoided mid-water lines.

At 11.30am, following considerable bubbling over the area baited with tiger nuts, I had a nice fast run and within one minute my first winter carp was in the net; a common of 20-12 which I recognized as one I'd caught in the autumn, because of a huge growth over an eye.

For the next two hours I was entertained by a big fish around the 30 pound mark which insisted on continually rolling about 15 feet out along the bank to my left. I hesitated to put a bait there at first — I don't really know why I did as I'm one to seize any opportunity — I suppose I was reluctant to move one of the 'long distance' rods because of the amount of fish that had shown earlier. Anyway, by the time I decided to put a bait there the fish disappeared, the fog came down and the rest of the day remained uneventful.

Nothing happened throughout the night, which didn't really surprise me for I've never caught a carp in foggy conditions. The air cleared at dawn and at eight o'clock I had a belting run on tiger nut but felt nothing on the strike. Before I could recast I had a run on the right hand rod finding the culprit to be a common of about eight pounds. This fish picked up a double tiger nut rig which I had re-positioned near the overhanging

willow in the shallows just before dark. At 9am I scattered six pouchfulls of tiger nuts over an area about six feet square exactly where the big fish had continually rolled the previous day. A piece of Spam about $\frac{1}{2}'' \times \frac{1}{4}''$ was mounted on a hair-rig to a fixed lead set up and this was carefully positioned in the middle of the free offerings. I had chosen Spam for three reasons; firstly, I wanted a very light bait which would lie on top of the silt and not get buried, secondly, I wanted a visual bait. I knew the carp would feed on the tigers sooner or later (they always did) and I wanted a bait amongst them that couldn't be missed. The third reason was that I wanted to confirm to myself that the Redmire carp would take anything — they had eaten everything else I'd tried so why not Spam? Feeling very confident I brewed a hot cup of tea and contentedly watched a Heron stalking its prey directly opposite me.

I didn't have to wait long before the piece of meat was taken and after playing the fish carefully for about ten minutes a big orange leather rolled into the net — undoubtedly the fish which had displayed the previous day. I immediately recognised the fish as the famous leather and knowing it was some fifty years old I handled it with the greatest possible care. I had seen the fish earlier in the season at 28-12 when Peter Springate caught it but it looked fatter this time and, knowing that all the fish weights had gone up by about one and a half pounds since the autumn I had high hopes that it might be a 'thirty'. As I slipped the fish into the weighing sling it uncannily lay perfectly still knowing full well what was happening, and I paused for a moment and felt a little sadness for the fish. My mind drifted for a second and I remembered an article by Len Arbery where he referred to this fish as the 'Mug of Redmire'. It seemed an unfair 'label' for such a lovely old carp — something about the fish was different — it was far from good looking but as I looked at its face and into its eyes I could sense it had a character of its own. Just think of its fifty years of life, and the pleasure it must have given anglers like Pete Climo, Chris Yates and Kevin Clifford, to name just a few of its captors. The next thing I remember was the scales reading 30 pounds two ounces. I was really pleased because I was beginning to think I'd never get a Redmire thirty after having so far caught 15 twenties with two weighing in at 29-12 and 29-13! I quickly put the fish into a keepsack and went to find Dave the farm hand. He kindly verified the weight for me, in fact he made it 30lb 4oz, and took some photographs before it was very carefully returned to its home.

I had no other action that day but at 12.30am I was awoken by another tremendously fast run on the right hand rod which was baited with two tiger nuts on two hairs (as described in an earlier session) and still positioned alongside the overhanging willow in the shallows. Strangely enough the fish, a mirror of 23-4, turned out to be another famous carp going by the name of 'Raspberry'.

The remainder of the session was rather hectic to say the least. However, space does not allow me to describe the full details only suffice to say that after losing a fish that morning in another swim a convoy of Land Rovers arrived and gangs of workmen unloaded their trailers and set about felling the telegraph poles, which are only ten feet from the water, with power saws. Despite having never seen so much disturbance at a carp lake before I wasn't too bothered and left for home in a happy mood.

Three weeks later I was at the pool again for my second winter session. I switched off the engine and as I rolled down the hill it struck me how different the pool looked. Winter had taken its effect and the place looked cold and bare. There were no leaves at all on the trees now and the water was a thick red colour due to large amounts of rainfall over the past week or so. Before looking round I decided to go straight to the hut to see how the other members had got on but discovered that no-one had been. This amazed me as I'd informed the following rota immediately after my successful last visit, but despite good conditions for nearly a fortnight nobody had bothered. Unfortunately this visit turned out to be my first blank at Redmire so I will just give brief details of the session. I fished the Willow swim, using three different baits — tiger nuts, Spam and a cream boilie. There was a heavy frost that night and I had only one take, which was probably a line bite. There were some bubblers about the next day, so I moved to the Stumps swim. Although I still felt confident there was no action except for a four inch twitch on Spam. There was another severe frost that night; $-10°$, and I couldn't see the other side of the lake for the mist. There was no action so I packed up at 2pm on the 27th after $51\frac{1}{2}$ hours without a fish.

I couldn't get back to the pool until early January as my previous rota had coincided with the two weeks around Christmas and it was one of the syndicate rules that we should not go there in that period. I could find no signs of fish on my recce and there were no entries in the book so I decided to start in the Willow swim. The water was quite heavily coloured but not red as on the previous visit; it was brown this time. It was mild and I felt confident and I didn't have to wait long for some action. In fact I had continual bites on all rods for the next 24 hours. It was frustrating at first because I kept striking at these weird bites, most of which were stop/start takes. I suspected eels to be the culprits as we'd had the same problems in the summer but I had always been told that eels were not active in midwinter. Eventually I retrieved a couple of baits with jaw marks across them and decided it must be eels. By 3pm the following day I'd had about 200 of these weird bites and it made no difference what bait was used so I moved to the Stumps swim as I was confident that conditions were good enough for carp to be feeding somewhere.

By late afternoon the wind blew very strongly towards the shallows with rain on and off but it remained quite mild. By 5pm it was dark, the wind had increased to gale force and it was all I could do to keep my gear on the ground. There was so much underwater drag that even several heavy indicators were pulled straight up to the butt so I fitted the lines into two drag clips on each rod. Despite this the lines kept coming out of the clips and runs followed. A couple of hours later branches started to fall off trees and the underwater drag was so strong that all the new weed growth was uprooted and this built up on the lines. The rods kept blowing off the rests and I was propping them up with all sorts of things. Continual recasting was necessary as each belting run had to be checked in case it was a fish. One of the runs turned out to be a three pound eel and I was particularly pleased as this proved to me that eels were to blame for the weird bites I'd been getting and it also proved that eels feed in January! I kept on striking every run and at 7.30pm the rod was almost torn from my grasp. It was pitch black, the wind so strong that I could hardly stand up and if that wasn't enough it was raining too. Fortunately the fish didn't put up much of a fight and was soon in the net. It was my old friend the common with a growth over one eye and I immediately returned the fish after recording a weight of 21-4.

I was absolutely worn out by the time dawn broke. I'd had no sleep the first night due to eels and none again the second night because of the gale. Finally, at about 8am the wind began to drop and I could sit back, sort my gear out and put the kettle on. A couple of hours had passed when I just heard a faint splash to my right and I stood up just in time to see a small flat spot rapidly disappearing amongst the rippled surface. I watched for a moment and no duck emerged so I cast a cream boilie there just in case. Half an hour later I had a slow run on that bait and struck into a very powerful fish. It fought extremely well and it wasn't until 30 minutes later that it was ready to net. Throughout the fight quite a bit of silkweed built up on the line until eventually the tip ring was gummed up solid. The line became tighter and tighter in the ring until eventually it threatened a breakage if I tried to retrieve any more line. There was no alternative but to put the rod down and hand line the fish the last few yards to the net. This manoeuvre succeeded and a nice big common rolled into the net. The hardship of the session was soon forgotten as the beautiful golden common tipped the scales at exactly 27 pounds. At 4pm I left for home — a tired but happy man.

After so many successful trips to Redmire I was obviously keen to get back and three weeks later I made my final journey to the pool — a session I will never forget. It was January 26th and the temperatures had been exceptionally high for the time of year.

To say I felt confident would be an understatement — I simply knew I was going to catch fish; there was no doubt in my mind. As soon as I arrived I had a quick look at the record book and once again, the last entry was my own which meant that still no other member had fished the pool since the end of October! For the first time ever I didn't bother to have a good look round the pool, I knew where the fish would be and I just wanted to get set up as soon as possible in the Stumps. Conditions were perfect; a light westerly wind blowing into the shallows, patchy cloud and very warm and as I set up two big fish rolled in front of me. The left hand rod was baited with a cream boilie on a fixed lead set up and fished over a carpet of tiger nuts in the same spot as I'd caught the big leather. The other rods were set up the same and once all the lines had settled I pulled off some slack and sat back to await events. I suppose I was over-confident as I expected a fish within the first couple of hours but it wasn't until 1.30pm that I had a run on the left hand rod. A lively 15 minute fight followed and an immaculate common of 26-8 was soon being admired on the bank. As with most Redmire carp its body shape was of perfect proportions and it looked brand new. I quickly popped the fish into a sack and secured it in front of the Evening Swim.

    I recast the left hand rod to exactly the same position and within five minutes my Heron buzzer was screeching again. The indicator whacked up against the rod and the line poured from the spool at an alarming rate. I picked the rod up, shut the bale arm and the compound taper carbon automatically took up its full fighting curve. There was no stopping this fish as far as the tackle was concerned — it swam with such power and speed that any attempt to turn it would have mean a breakage. I just hung on as the carp made its way up towards the dam about 50 yards away. Eventually it got there and it had no alternative but

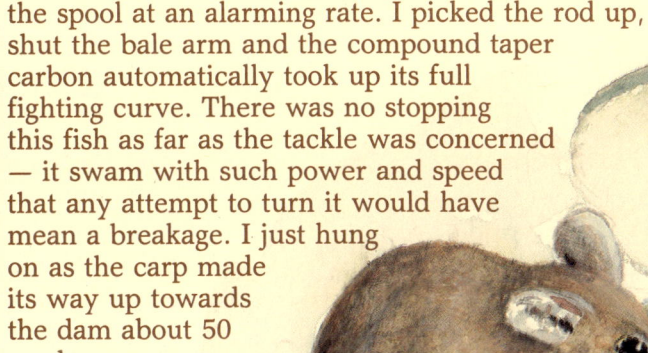

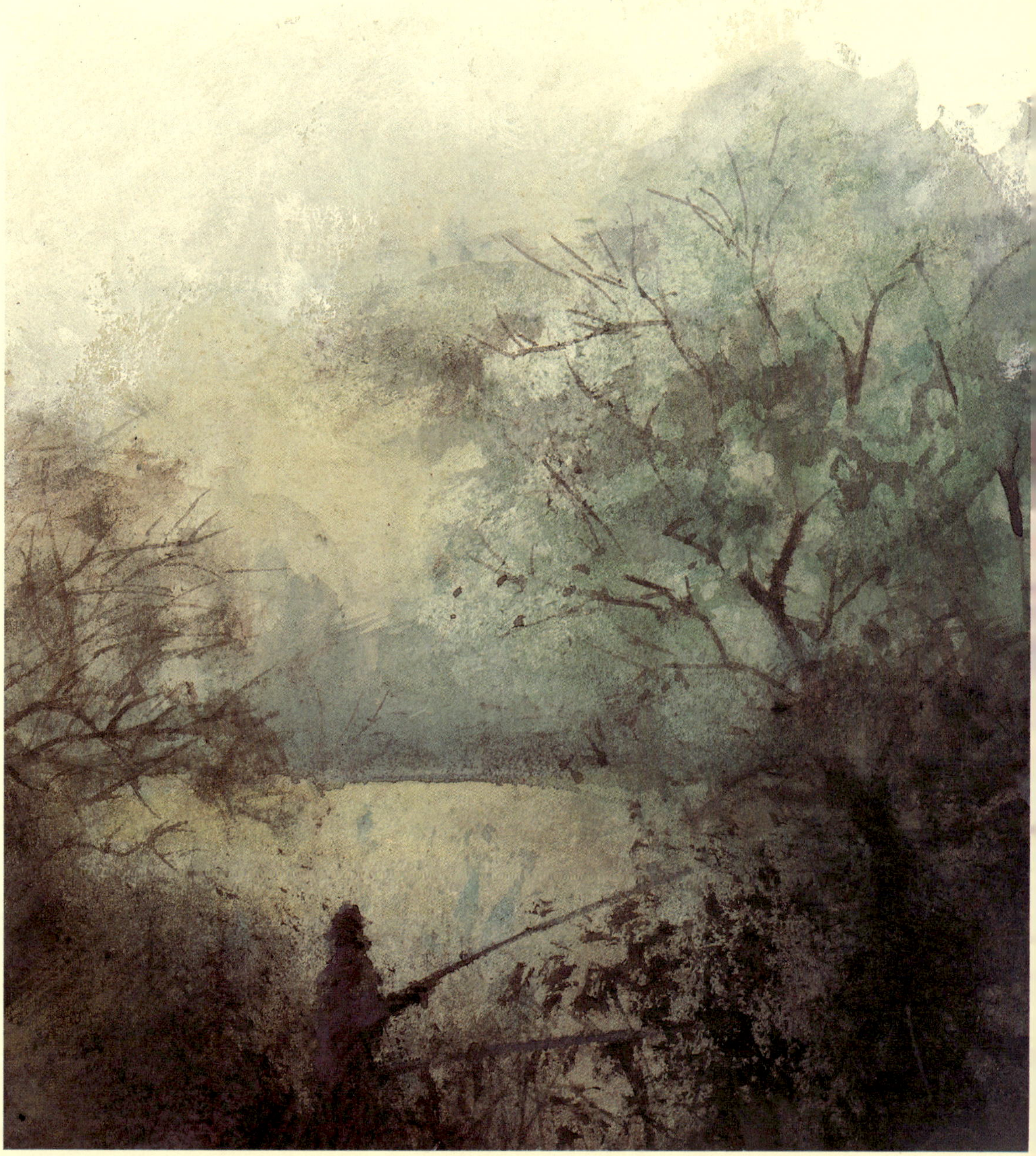

to turn right and swim along the dam wall. The fish was certainly determined to keep its distance from me for after swimming close to the whole length of the dam it made its way along the margins on the opposite bank. Eventually I managed to coax it across the lake back to my swim but I knew it wasn't beaten so I slackened the clutch a little. That turned out to be a wise move because just as I got the carp near the net it turned and powered off along the left hand margins again. The two pound test curve rod was bent alarmingly as the fish made its second 50 yard run. Again it turned at the dam wall and followed its previous path. In all it took me almost half an hour to land the fish and even then I don't think it was ready and my arm was really aching. As I lifted the fish out I was a little disappointed to see it was another common, because I prefer mirrors, but nevertheless it was a really good looking fish weighing in at 25-4.

The following hour was spent worrying about how to get some decent pictures of the brace. There was no one about and I didn't want to pester the farm hand again so I photographed the pair of commons on my own using a tripod and remote release. Holding two big lively fish and trying to pose suitably whilst operating the remote proved to be more than difficult but it was all I could do in the circumstances.

At 12.45am the left hand rod was in action yet again. I don't remember the run, shutting the bale arm or striking; I was so tired due to only two hours sleep the previous night. The first thing I knew was that it was the middle of the night and I was holding a rod bent double. Non-carp anglers will find that amazing but having spent two nights a week carp fishing for ten years one can easily perform such tasks whilst three quarters asleep! The result — a 21-4 common which I opted to return immediately, saving another fiasco trying to take pictures.

By dawn the wind had increased in strength to gale force and although my umbrella was set up at the correct angle an opposite gust of wind turned the brollie inside out and snapped the pole clean in two. The lower half of the pole still remains at Redmire! Despite it being an expensive 50" model only one week old I wasn't at all bothered, after all it was a small price to pay for three twenty pound plus commons.

The wind remained strong all morning which I knew the Redmire carp disliked — they usually preferred it calm or with a light breeze but my confidence was restored at mid-day when it dropped a little. I climbed one of the poplar trees to my right and after 30 minutes of peering into the water I could just make out the water to be slightly coloured about 15 feet out and about three quarters of the way towards the Evening Swim from my pitch. I reeled the right hand rod in, changed the set-up to a bolt rig with a boilie and cast it to the spot where I'd suspected fish to be feeding. A quick swap round of the rods now made this the left hand rod. An hour later, at 4pm, I had a run on the left hand rod and the fight that followed was terrific. That fish did everything the twenty five pounder did and more — at one stage it tried to swim out of the outflow and for at least five minutes the rod was held under the water up to the reel to keep the line out of the trees and bushes along the whole of the bank I was fishing. Thirty-five minutes after hooking I pulled the big fish over the net and I could see it was a very big common. As I lifted it ashore I knew what I'd caught straight away — a fish of a lifetime and the dream of all carp anglers — a thirty pound common. As I removed the size 2 barbless hook, which was neatly embedded in the bottom lip, I could feel my heart thumping like mad and I knew this was what carp fishing is all about — the sleepless nights, the incredible determination and suffering which goes into carp fishing — this was what it was for. I'd caught plenty of carp bigger than this one but this was special, very special. Its body was exceptionally deep for a Redmire fish and it was almost the colour of a goldfish. I weighed the fish accurately and although it didn't weigh quite as much as I thought it would, at 30-8 I wasn't complaining. I wrote the following in my diary. "Fantastic session. I have passed being amazed — just can't understand it. Why in January can you do something you can't do at any time in the summer?"

    I fished a further night and day but had no other action and I left at 4.30pm. That was to be my last session at Redmire and in a way I'm glad I didn't return for a final fling in March because the result would almost certainly have been an anticlimax after such an historic catch. Left as it is my memories will remain sweet ones.

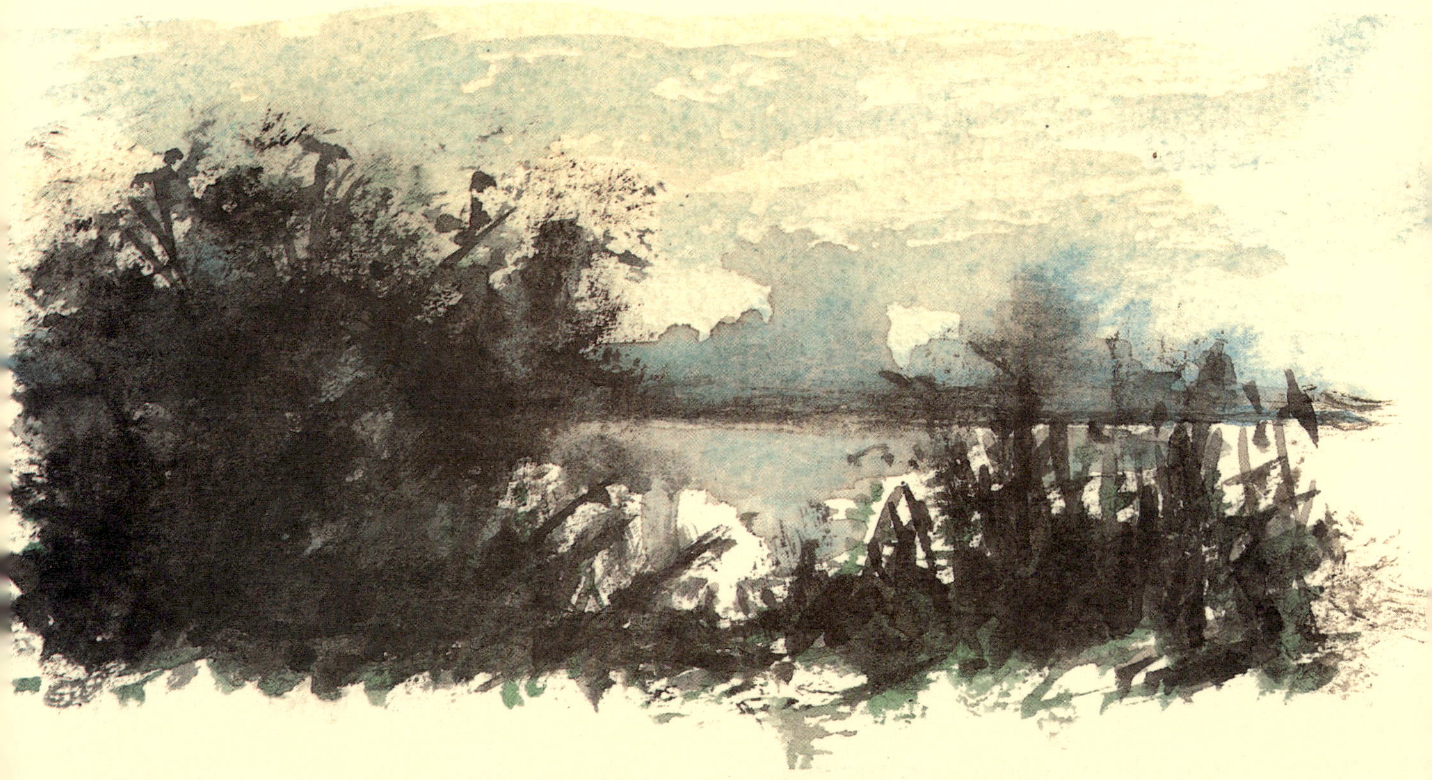

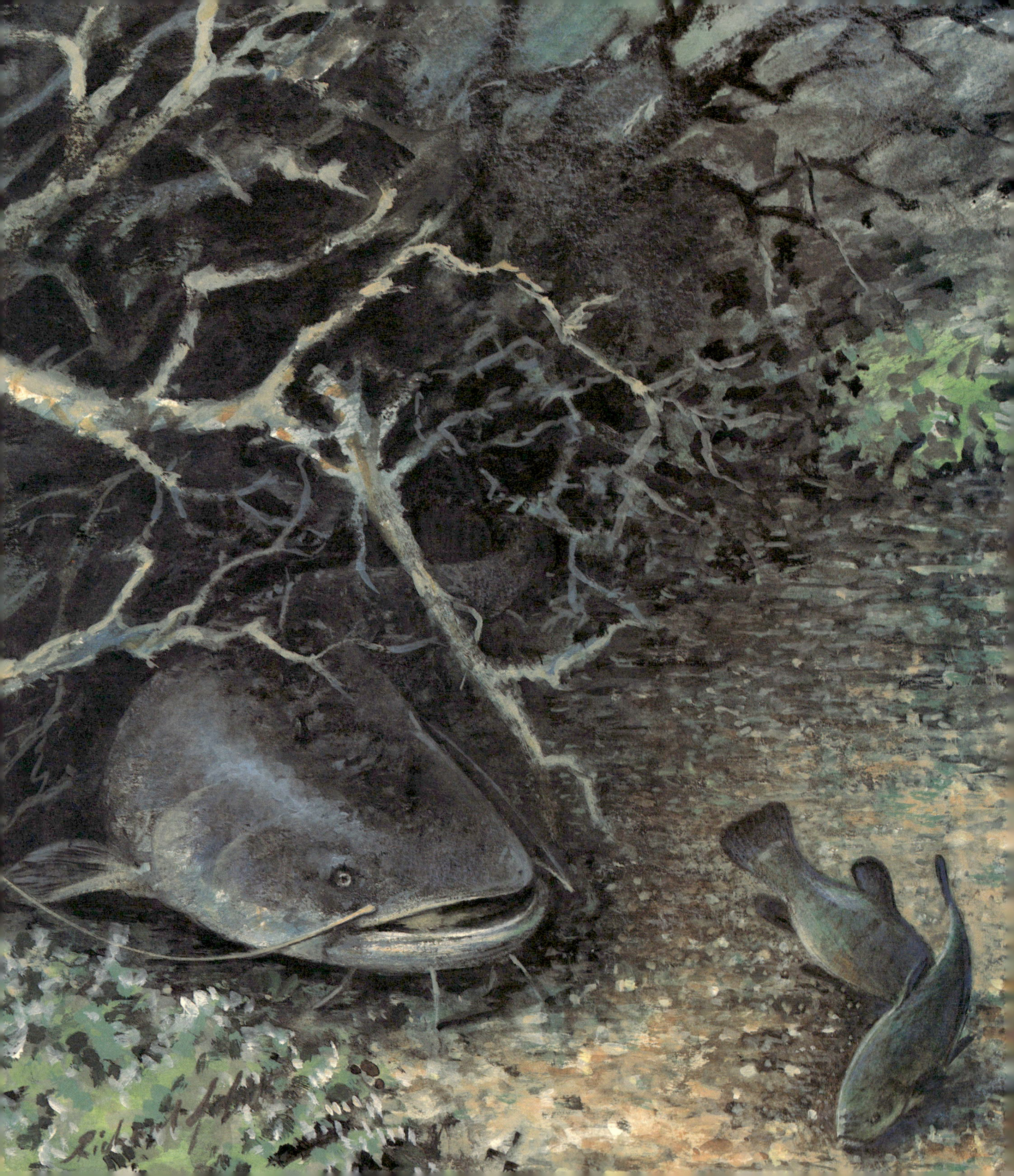

Failure or Success?

After about two years of fishing for catfish I had caught about 50, so I was looking for a new challenge; a water which might contain a very big fish. My attention was drawn to several waters but especially the Tring Reservoirs which seemed to contain some of the mystery I was seeking. Marsworth had been stocked by the second Lord Rothschild with a small handful of big fish up to 28 pounds about 80 years ago — in 1906.

Apart from a genuine capture of a four pound catfish in 1928, which verified that a breeding population had evolved, nothing was heard of these fish until 1934, when a five foot catfish, estimated at between 35-40 pounds was found dead. (A photograph of this fish was published in the Catfish Conservation Group's magazine *Whiskers 2*). In 1943, two other catfish, one of which was said to weigh about 50lbs, were also found dead. As it has been proved on the continent that *Silurus glanis* can live to at least 60 years of age it is not unreasonable to assume that those found dead were some of the original stock.

There appeared to be no more verified catfish reports from Marsworth until 1983, when an angler accidentally caught some small ones on worms. Bob Baldock and I believed that there were great possibilities here; if there were now small catfish in this 25 acre water, there had been catfish in the reservoir for nearly 80 years, they had bred and there could quite possibly be some very big parent fish present. Although the record fish of 43½lbs had been caught from Wilstone, this fish was almost certainly an illegal transfer, as only Marsworth had been officially stocked.

Although we were intrigued by genuine stories of huge fish taking hooked tench at Wilstone, I thought this rich, clear lake might be too difficult because it probably contained very few 'cats'. I also believed that catfish could have done better in Marsworth, which appeared to be shallower and warmer and seemed to contain much more food fish.

In the close season of 1984, we joined the Tring night syndicate, and made our plans for the season. Since catfish grow to enormous sizes in other countries we felt convinced that we should prepare ourselves for the possibility of hooking fish of up to 60lbs, and possibly much more, which we wanted to make sure that we landed. Since Marsworth is over 200 yards across at its widest point, with the far bank inaccessible as it is a Nature Reserve, we reasoned that reels which would hold 300 yards of at least 15lb line were required. I decided on Zebco Sterling 7050 sea reels and Bob managed to obtain a pair of very large Mitchells. I also had a special landing net made up by Simpsons of Turnford, which had five foot arms and a very narrow front which would help to prevent a very long catfish from sliding backwards over the front cord of the net. Apart from these special items, all the rest of the tackle was heavy carp gear.

Since members of the night syndicate were allowed to use a boat at night for baiting up, I bought an inflatable dinghy.

We thought a lot about bait, as we wanted to use something which was fairly cheap, easily obtainable, which we could bait up with in the close season, and which no other fish was likely to take. We finally decided on squid, with which I, and some friends, had caught a lot of catfish on other waters. As far as I know, I was the first angler to use squid to catch catfish so it was an obvious choice for me, and Bob agreed.

Early that close season we spent several days surveying the water and drawing a plan of the bottom with the depths marked on it. Marsworth is a very busy day-ticket water so we decided to fish an area well away from the most popular swims. As we had found that the water varied from 2 feet to 12 feet deep we chose to start by fishing six to eight feet of water which we thought would warm up quickly and would most likely be visited by catfish. We bought £300 worth of frozen Calamarie squid which was stored in a large chest freezer especially purchased by Bob and kept in his garage.

It will give some idea of how determined we were when I say that our expenses were already more than £500 — and we hadn't yet started fishing!

Throughout the second half of the close season, for a period of six weeks we baited up alternately, three times a week with the whole squid — which meant for me, a round trip of 70 miles each time it was my turn. Since we initially wanted to fish an area about 20 yards out, and squid is too soft to throw very far we froze the bait in blocks, each with a stone in it to make it sink, and on each trip we put in about 10lbs of squid. By the time June 16th came round, we were very confident that catfish must have been sampling the squid, which has an exceptionally strong smell and which we were convinced, when introduced regularly in the same area, would draw the fish to the bait from all over the lake.

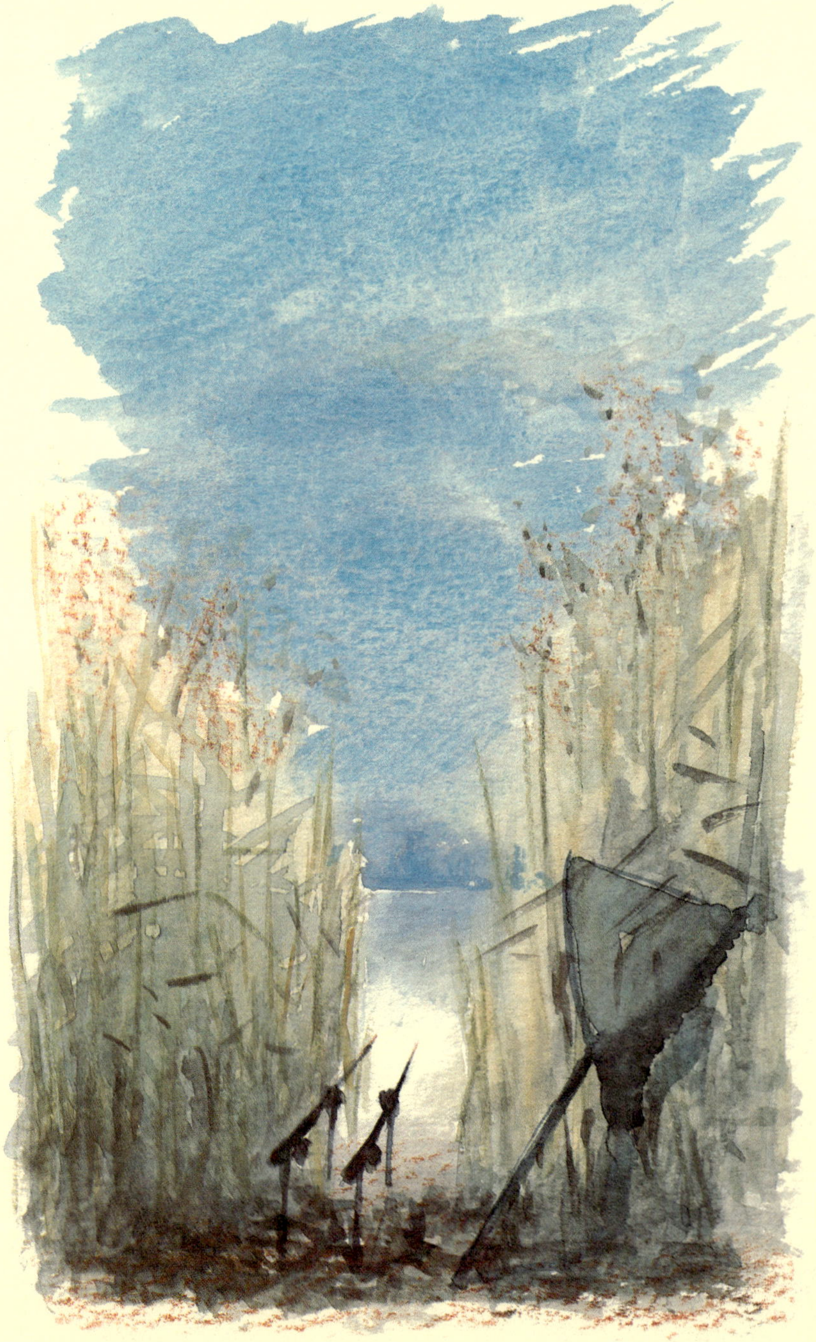

For the majority of the summer we fished almost every area of the lake three nights a week; we even waded out to a large reed island, cut swims and fished areas which are normally inaccessible, and at one time we were fishing at a range of 200 yards — by taking out two baits at a time in the boat and dropping them over the side; we really tried.

Sadly we failed; our only achievement was catching the first ever catfish intentionally from the Tring group of reservoirs. I had four and Bob had one — they weighed from 2½ pounds to 4lbs. These were all caught on small pieces of freelined squid despite the fact that we'd tried many different baits. To make matters worse that season I took a few days off from Marsworth in September to fish Claydon with Leo Westdrop, who was over from Holland for a trip that I had promised him, so I had to go and in that short time I caught catfish of 30¼lbs, 29½lbs, 24½lbs and 13lbs. What a contrast; all that effort for so little at Marsworth, and all these big fish at Claydon for so little effort. Which was the biggest achievement? To me it was the Tring fish, small though they were but many people might not agree. In fact, I had those Claydon fish with so little effort that it put me off the place a bit — I haven't yet returned.

It soon got around amongst catfish anglers and members of the CCG that we were on Marsworth, and everyone was waiting for us to succeed — and some didn't believe we were not catching. We had plenty of visits from catfish anglers but not one would give it a proper try. If we had caught a few decent fish I've no doubt it would be a popular catfish venue thereafter!

One day I shall go back and try again as I still believe there are a few big catfish in Marsworth. Why shouldn't there be? Those little fish must have parents — somewhere. Perhaps they were in about the only place we didn't try — under the causeway bushes about a rod length out in 12 feet of water. We shall never know unless some other catfish anglers take it on — and I dearly wish they would, as I would like to see someone get one of these monsters of Marsworth — even if I didn't.

I suppose partly because of its comparative rarity, the catfish must be regarded as the most mysterious fish in this country. Its fantastic fight, and the size to which it might grow, makes it fascinating as well as mysterious, and because of this I should like to put down just a few of my thoughts on fishing for catfish.

One of the problems of trying to catch catfish is that there are long periods when the fish simply don't feed, and often nothing the angler can do will make them feed. This means that you are spending — or rather wasting much of your time which would be better spent somewhere else; I've always said that catfishing is the best waste of time I know! Unlike most fish, the catfish has a stomach, so it doesn't need to feed frequently. The trouble is, how can you find out when to be fishing for them? If you can't, then there is no alternative but to spend long hours on the banks, waiting for the feeding spells. It has been proved on the Continent that catfish become highly active when the water temperature is over 80°F, but since this rarely occurs in this country, there is no way the situation will change.

As mentioned in *Golden Summer with the Neglected Giant,* a very heavy baiting at Claydon did produce some response, but this is not a typical water, on other waters where I have tried pre-baiting I had no measureable success at all. I would never embark on a heavy pre-baiting scheme for catfish again; it appears to be a waste of time. However, some baiting whilst fishing is definitely worthwhile.

In my opinion, once the catfish does become active, it throws all caution to the wind and covers the area very quickly, searching for food and taking baits at any depth. At Claydon it is not unusual for a fish to get caught more than once in a day, although it has not been taken in previous weeks, so it's obvious that being caught does not disturb them much. For example, at my own water, Withy Pool, I once had 4 runs in three hours one night in late October. The first run I struck and made no contact. On the second run I hooked and pulled out of a powerful fish after about half a minute's fight. The third run I intended to leave a while before striking (I normally strike instantly) because of what happened on the previous two runs, but after taking about 15 yards of line the fish dropped the bait before I struck. An instant strike on the fourth run produced a very hard fighting 11 pounder. This fish had a bleeding tear on its side, and I am sure that it was the same fish which had taken my raw liver bait every time and on one occasion I had foul hooked it. I have had similar experiences elsewhere which have led me to the same conclusion.

On other waters I have heard of foul-hooked catfish being returned and then caught again within a few hours. This proves that when catfish are feeding they are quite insensitive to being hooked and caught, but if they are not on the feed, usually nothing will affect them.

Another difference between catfish and carp is that catfish don't appear to be able to detect the line over their lips, but they are resistance-shy; a heavy indicator or any other form of resistance will often make them eject the bait. The only exception I have found to this is when using a bare hook set-up, such as the hair rig, in conjunction with a fixed lead.

I've tried many different sorts of rigs; hair rigs, bolt rigs and most other types, but in my opinion freelining is easily the best method for catfishing using a heavy braided hooklink. With some baits, such as squid, whelks, mussels, liver etc, it is worth using the hair rig to prevent hooks being struck into the bait. I have seen many catfish missed and lost because of this common problem. When I'm not using the hair rig I am very careful to mount the bait in such a way that the point, barb and bend of the hook is exposed and that it cannot pull back into the bait. I do however think it is an advantage to cover the hook's shank where possible. Choice of bait is particularly important, as catfish rarely take some baits such as boilies, for example. I am not saying that you will not catch them on boilies; as mentioned in an earlier chapter I have caught them on meaty boilies but I do know of several carp waters which contain a reasonable head of 'cats' yet they are very rarely caught on boilies despite the fact that anglers are using them day and night all summer long. It is quite obvious from these results that the bait has to be right and that you cannot 'wean' catfish onto any old bait by simply introducing large quantities over a long period. I am sure that catfish sample every type of bait, and that the first time a catfish comes across a new bait it investigates it thoroughly, and often leaves it if it doesn't find it acceptable, but that once you do find the right bait for the water, stick to it, and the catfish will take it freely.

Catfish hunt their food mainly by smell, and taste is achieved by use of feelers, body and mouth, but I am sure they can also detect vibration through the water, the type of vibration produced by a livebait, for example. For this reason, if I am going to use a fish bait, I would always use Bob Baldock's livebait set up, as described in *Whiskers 4*. Apart from a livebait, I would now only use worms, mussels, squid or raw liver: those five baits have proved to be the best in my experience — most of the rest don't seem to be as good, although I have had catfish on many different baits.

In most lakes it has been found that if the water is clear, the fish tend to feed almost entirely at night, whilst in opaque waters they often feed during daytime. Whilst this is not an invariable rule it is one which almost always applies and the only exception to this that I have seen is in clear, weedy waters. The reason for this seems to be that catfish require 'cover' of some kind when they feed, so they must be able to detect whether the water is clear or opaque, presumably by eyesight. It has been said by some people that they eyesight of a catfish is very poor, but it certainly does seem that it is good enough to detect varied light intensity and I should think that this is the main role of the catfish's eyes. I have watched catfish feeding on live fish and they are quite inefficient, often missing completely and acting as if they're blind; this again backs up my belief that vibration plays a big part in the catfishes detection. I have many other interesting thoughts and beliefs about the behaviour of the wels but I will not bore you any longer as no doubt some of them are completely wrong — that's what makes this fish so fascinating.

It seems to me that catfish in this country have a great future, especially if they become more widespread, as I hope they will. The Catfish Conservation Group, which I helped to found, is working hard in this direction, and also assisting with attempts to breed the fish in this country. I urge all big fish anglers to try to catch themselves one of these remarkable, hard fighting fish; I know no-one who has done so who in any way regrets the time spent to put one of these fascinating monsters on the bank.

There is no species more interesting in this country or anywhere else.

© Kevin Maddocks 1986

First published 1986 by

Beekay Publishers Ltd.,
Withy Pool
Bedford Road
Henlow Camp
Bedfordshire
England SG16 6EA.

ISBN 0 947674 06 3

Design and production
The Kingfisher Organisation
20 Beaufort Gardens,
Ascot, Berks.

Printed in England